Journey of a Betrayed Hero

Volume 2

Written by Brandon Varnell
Illustrations by Aisoretto

Journey of a Betrayed Hero, Volume 2
Copyright © 2019 Brandon Varnell
Illustration Copyright © 2019 Aisoretto
All rights reserved.

To see Brandon Varnell's other works, or to ask for permission to use his works, visit him at www.varnell-brandon.com, facebook at www.facebook.com/AmericanKitsune, twitter at www.twitter.com/BrandonbVarnell, Patreon at www.Patreon.com/BrandonVarnell, and instagram at www.instagram.com/brandonbvarnell.

ISBN-13: 978-0-9989942-5-3

CONTENT

If you would like to know when Brandon Varnell releases a new book, please sign up for his mailing list at https://www.varnell-brandon.com/mailing-list.

PROLOGUE - THE HERO IS A TRAITOR

It was late at night as Alice tossed and turned on her bed. Sweat had broken out on her forehead, and her lips twisted as if she was in pain.

Her sleep was often plagued with nightmares, visions of what happened in the past, present, and what could happen future. Foresight was a powerful magic indeed. However, it was relatively useless for real life situations, and it generally only activated while she slept.

That night, as with most nights, her dreams featured Jacob, the hero who'd saved her kingdom and vanished from the palace after forsaking his title. This dream happened the same way every dream had. He would appear before her, his face older, his body more mature. The expression that he wore reflected the pain he felt, and his eyes were accusing daggers that knifed her through her heart.

"You betrayed me," he would say.

"I didn't!" she denied.

"You left me alone. When I needed help, you weren't there. When the nobles tried to use me, you refused to so much as lift a finger. You promised me that we would always be together, but you weren't there when I needed you the most. You betrayed me."

"That's not true! I wanted to help, but my... my hands were tied! Please, you have to believe me!"

"Traitor."

"Stop it..."

"Traitor."

"Please stop..."

"You're a traitor."

"I said stop it!!" Alice screamed as she shot up in bed. She took several deep breaths, gasping lungfuls of air. Glancing around, she recognized the cream walls, splendid decor, and beautifully crafted vaulted ceiling. It was her bedroom.

Alice pressed a hand to her face, grimacing as it came away slick with sweat. In fact, her entire body was covered in sweat, and her nightgown was caked to her skin. When she looked down, she saw that her clothes had been so thoroughly soaked that her breasts were visible through the fabric.

When will this nightmare end?

It probably wouldn't end. Not ever. That was the conclusion that she'd reached years ago after Jacob had left. It would plague her to the end of her days, a constant reminder of how she had failed to protect the kingdom's hero. Her hero.

The sound of movement alerted her to the other person in the room. A woman dressed in a white nightgown appeared before her, Listy, her maid and best friend.

"Are you having trouble sleeping again, My Lady?" Listy asked.

"It was just the same nightmare as usual," Alice said, as if that would assure her maid.

"That nightmare again." Listy sighed. "I feel like you are far too hung up on the hero."

"It is not necessarily that I am hung up on him," Alice admonished. "It is my failure to protect him after he'd done so much for my people that continues to bother me."

Perhaps it had been due to his age, or maybe it was because she had been young as well, but when Jacob had been summoned to this world, she felt like she'd finally understood how heroes felt.

Every hero in their history was one that had been summoned from another world. They were torn from their homes, forced to fight for a people they didn't know, and at the end of it all, the only thing that awaited them was either death or a life of loneliness. However, she only understood this fact after Jacob had left.

"Jacob saved our kingdom, but I couldn't do anything to save him," Alice continued.

"It is regrettable what happened to Lord Jacob," Listy allowed. "However, as our queen, you cannot devote all of your time and attention to one man. It would have been a greater disservice to his actions if you had not helped your people after the war ended."

Alice felt a sardonic smile tugging at her lips. "Somehow, I don't think Jacob would feel the same way."

"That may be so, but that is how it is. In the end, your loyalty is to your people, not to a single person."

This was not the first time she and Listy had this conversation. They'd spoken of her feelings many times, and every time, Listy said the same thing. It was not her concern. Her loyalty was to her people. She knew that, of course. After all, she had chosen her people over Jacob, but that didn't make it easier to accept how her neglect had pushed him away. It didn't change how she'd allowed the nobles to abuse him.

"Let's take a bath, Listy," Alice said. "I feel disgusting."

"As you wish, My Lady."

The bathhouse was a large room that could have easily seated forty people, though only she and Listy used it. A large pool filled with steaming water sat in the center of the room. After undressing in the changing room, Alice and Listy wandered over to the left wall, where there was a stool along with a bucket.

She sat down on the stool. Listy grabbed the bucket, filled it up at the pool, and then came back and poured the hot water onto Alice's head. Her maid did this two more times before beginning to wash her body.

"I am always jealous of how soft your skin is," Listy commented as she ran a loofa over Alice's arms.

"Your skin is just as soft as mine," Alice contradicted. "And let us not forget another area where you shine that I am lacking in."

"If you are referring to my chest, then that only makes sense," Listy said. "I am older than you, and you are still growing. Give it time."

Alice sighed. "If you say so."

"I do say so."

While Alice did feel a little bit of envy toward Listy's enviable bust, it was not like she was lacking in that department. She knew she had a large chest for her age. At the same time, she remembered how Jacob had once found himself mesmerized by her maid's chest and felt a flash of envy toward the other woman.

After the two of them finished helping each other wash up, they waded into the pool, stepping down the marble steps and entering the sitting area. Heat rose all around them. Steam wafted off the water's surface. Alice sighed as she leaned her head back and tried to forget her worries, if only for these next few minutes. Soon, she would have to return to the life of a queen, she would hold the lives of millions of people in her hands, and their weight would be crushing. However, at this moment, just for now, she was merely a simple seventeen-year-old girl taking a bath with her best friend.

It was sad that all good things must come to an end. Alice and Listy eventually redressed and wandered down the hall. Night had turned into early morning, so Alice decided to grab something to eat.

She and Listy traveled into the kitchens, where her head maid was already up and wandering around. Dressed in nothing but her nightgown, Alice sat down on a tall stool in front of the table normally used to prepare ingredients. Her bare feet couldn't reach the floor.

"Mornin', Your Highness." The head maid didn't even look away from her work as she greeted Alice.

"Morning, Melinda."

"I'm guessing you want the same thing as usual?"

"Yes, please."

The "same as usual" was actually just simple oats and milk. Alice enjoyed simple breakfasts over extravagant ones. She had enough lavish meals prepared for lunch and dinner, especially when she was meeting with a member of the nobility. She didn't need to deal with that in the morning.

While she and Listy enjoyed their breakfast, the door to the kitchens opened, and Bayard walked in.

"I knew I'd find you here when I noticed that you weren't in your room," Bayard said.

"You were looking for me?" Alice asked.

"Yes, there's been a... a situation that requires your attention."

Alice, realizing that whatever had made Bayard search her out must have been grave, sighed and pushed away her food. It looked like she wouldn't get to be a simple girl as much as she would have liked this morning.

"What happened?" she asked, adopting her role as queen.

Bayard coughed into his hand. "Reports coming in are varied—however, there are three things that we have confirmed. The first is that we located who we believe is the thief, though she somehow managed to escape."

"So in the end, even our paladins couldn't catch her?"

"Do not be so quick to blame the paladins for this, your majesty," Bayard said. "There were extenuating circumstances. The city the thief was discovered in, Tallus Caelum, was attacked by an unknown person. That person destroyed nearly one-tenth of the city."

Alice paled, while Melinda and even Listy gasped. "W-what?"

Bayard sighed and rubbed his face. "We're not sure who, but one-tenth of Tallus Caelum was destroyed by what reports claim was a woman of unknown origins."

"Unknown origins?" Listy questioned.

"It was night, and there was too much chaos happening to get a proper glimpse of her. However, a rumor has spread that she was a member of the Dark Clan."

"The Dark Clan." Alice placed her head in her hands. She could already feel the headache this situation would give her. "We haven't heard a peep from them in nearly three years. Why would they suddenly appear now?"

"Your guess is as good as mine," Bayard said, shrugging. "Anyway, there is something else that you should know."

"And that is?"

"It seems the person who fought against this woman was none other than Jacob."

"Jacob?!" Alice almost fell off her seat. "Where is he? Is he still in Tallus Caelum? How is he?"

Bayard raised a hand for silence. Alice frowned, but she knew he wouldn't have done something that would have normally been considered rude for no reason.

"Unfortunately, Your Majesty, Jacob is not in good shape. When he was found by Caslain, he was on death's door. I've been told that his wounds are horrific."

"Is he going to be okay?" she asked.

"We believe so," Bayard said. "His wounds have been healing rapidly. They were healing even before our healers got to him. The reports said that he should recover in a few days."

Leaning back in her chair, Alice placed a hand over her chest. Her heart was beating harder than a pair of bongo drums being repeatedly pounded on.

"That's good."

"There is something else that you should know," Bayard said before she could become secure in this new knowledge. "Jacob was seen with two other people, women who are also from the Dark Clan. We now have evidence that Jacob was aiding the person who stole the gate key. He might be a traitor to the crown."

Alice had gone through many hardships. Her mother had died when she was young, and her father had followed on her twelfth birthday, forcing her to assume the role of queen before she was ready. Every day she fought against the nobles and the White Council, who sought to undermine her authority. Despite all this, she had remained strong, beating back the nobles with their flagrant desires to line their pockets with coin, and forcing the White Council to adopt her policies that would aid the people instead of themselves.

However, in that moment, Alice could have sworn her heart had broken. She didn't blame Jacob. She blamed herself.

Alice wondered if things might have been different if she had been there for Jacob when he needed her the most.

CHAPTER 1 - FAR APART BUT STILL TOGETHER

Enyo opened her eyes. The first thing she saw was a canopy of trees over her head. They blocked out the stars and night sky. Heat washed across her face, which alerted her to the fire that was crackling merrily away right next to her.

Sitting up, Enyo observed her surroundings. She was in what looked like a makeshift camp. Of course, she called it a camp, but that was a polite term to describe it. It was, in actuality, nothing but a small clearing with a fire. There was nothing else there—not even Fellis.

"Fellis?" she called out, though part of her was scared to do so. She nearly shrieked when something snapped, like a foot stepping on a twig. Swinging her head around, Enyo prepared for trouble, yet no trouble was forthcoming, and Fellis stepped out from several trees and into the fire's light.

"Enyo," she said. "I'm pleased to see you're awake."

"I'm glad you're awake too," Enyo nearly cried. "I don't remember anything that happened after falling into that river, but I do remember you being knocked unconscious. I was worried you'd drown."

Fellis's face shifted into an ugly grimace. "I am sorry about that. While we were falling, one of the drake riders attacked us. I blocked the spell, but it knocked me out."

"I'm just glad you're alright," Enyo admitted.

Smiling, Fellis sat down. "I am also glad for that."

A moment of silence fell upon them. Enyo stared into the crackling fire, her thoughts a whirlwind of activity. So much had happened in Tallus Caelum, and she hadn't had any time to put her thoughts in order. She wanted to know where they were, what happened to Tallus Caelum, and whether or not Jacob was safe.

"There hasn't been any word from Jacob," Fellis said suddenly, as if she'd somehow read Enyo's mind. "However, that's not so surprising. Given what happened to us, even if he defeated Lust and escaped, he wouldn't be able to find us unless he knew exactly what happened. He could be in the next town over and we wouldn't know it."

"I guess that's true." Enyo sighed as she drew her knees up to her chest. A thought soon occurred to her, causing her to look at Fellis. "Speaking of what happened to us, do you know where we are?"

"I have not been able to figure out where we are exactly, but I believe that we are a little more than two or three weeks travel from Alyssium."

"Alyssium, huh?"

Alyssium was the capital of Terrasole, and the home of Avant Heim, the royal castle where the otherworld gate was located. She'd heard the stories about it. Supposedly, Alyssium was a paradise on earth. The roads were said to have been paved with gold, and the houses were covered in flowers. Water flowed freely, food was plentiful, and the people were happy. Well, those were the stories anyway.

"In either event, we should eat and rest while we still can," Fellis said. "Tomorrow, we'll head out. I discovered a road while searching the area. It should lead to a town, where we can get a new map and plot a course for Alyssium."

Enyo nodded. "I understand."

As they ate the fish that Fellis had caught and cooked, Enyo looked up and wondered what Jacob was doing.

High above them, the stars shone like phosphorous lights.

***

Consciousness was slow to return to Jacob. His body felt heavy, weighed down, and exhausted. This didn't surprise him, much as he would have liked it to have been otherwise. His battle with that woman, Lust, had taken a toll on his body. Her last attack would have killed him if he hadn't ramped up the power of his energy barrier at the last second.

Jacob didn't open his eyes at first, but instead tried to get a feel for his location through his other senses. The bed that he was lying on was soft—softer than anything he'd felt in a long time. Cool air caressed his skin, yet he could tell from the warmth showering him that there was a window with sunlight spilling in. Wherever he was, it was ritzier than any place he'd been to in a long time.

Finally, he opened his eyes. A canopy hung over his head, soft and sheer, draped over the posts of his bed with an artistry that made him think someone had way too much time on their hands. He looked to the left. Then he looked right. The walls were cream, decorated with lovely columns and artwork interspersed. He saw landscape paintings and a few small statues. Above the canopy of his bed loomed a vaulted ceiling with a painting of a man heroically holding a sword as he battled against the Dark Clan.

"This is... Avant Heim?" he muttered, too tired to be shocked, but awake enough to realize that he should not be here.

"That is correct," a voice said.

Jacob looked to his left, at the woman who was standing there. When did she arrive? He didn't know. She had appeared without warning. She wore a black and white dress with numerous frills and a bodice that helped push up her chest. With her hands clasped together and her expression composed, she presented the picturesque image of what most people imagined when they thought of maids.

"Listy," he muttered. "It's been a long time."

"That it has," Listy replied. "I see you are in good health."

Jacob snorted. "If you consider being almost killed and then brought back to a place you never wished to see again 'good health,' then yes, I suppose I am."

"You are a lot more sarcastic than the last time I saw you."

"Thank you for letting me know that. I had no idea."

It had been a long time since Jacob had been to Avant Heim, three years, in fact. It had been his desire to never return to this place again. For him to be here now meant that someone must have found him in Tallus Caelum after the battle and brought him here. While there was no evidence to support his theory, he suspected that Caslain was the one responsible for this.

"I see that you still feel resentment toward Queen Alice," Listy commented, her tone cold.

"Resentment?" Jacob chuckled, but there was no humor in it. "Is that what you call it? Sorry, but resentment isn't what I feel."

"Then what is it?" Listy inquired.

"Apathy."

He and Listy stared at each other for a long time, and he could feel the way her gaze tried to pierce the veil he'd thrown over his emotions. She was looking for cracks in his calm. If there was even a slip up in his demeanor, she would detect it and use it against him. That was the kind of person Listy was.

"So I see," she said at last. "Please wait here, Lord Jacob. I was ordered to inform Queen Alice of when you healed."

Jacob tried to raise his arm, but he was too tired for even that. While his wounds had healed, his body had still taken a beating. It would be awhile before he was strong enough to start moving again. It would be longer still before he could think of escaping.

"Sure. Not like I have much of a choice."

"Thank you. I will return shortly. If you need anything, there are two guards standing at the door," she said, dropping a subtle reminder not to do something stupid because he was being watched.

Jacob said nothing. Listy left, the door slowly closing behind her.

***

The day after Enyo woke up, she and Fellis traveled down a dirt road to the nearest village. It was a small town. Enyo didn't even know its name, or if it even had a name. Wood buildings, plain designs, only a few hundred people at most, it was nothing like Tallus Caelum, or even Altus and Albany.

"We need to find a place to stay the night," Fellis said as they walked down the dirt road. "After that, we'll need to gather information."

"Right," Enyo agreed, though most of her attention was focused on the people around them. Everyone was looking at her and Fellis. It made her uncomfortable, but more than that...

Why are there only men?

It was something that she had noticed the moment they walked in, but there were only men in this village. Old men, young men, boys... there wasn't a single woman in sight. It gave her the chills for some reason.

"Who should we talk to to get information from?" Enyo asked.

"Let's see if there's a village chief or someone of similar standing," Fellis said.

It took a lot of asking around to get anywhere—most of the men seemed wary of them. If it wasn't for Fellis's Mind Manipulation, they probably would have never gotten anywhere.

The chief's home was not a home at all, but a bar. It was an old place that showed its age in the worn out wooden tiles and the faded appearance of the tables. There was little light. Enyo could see where several fairy lamps had been at one point, but no fairies made their homes there anymore. They were just empty lamps.

Fellis strode toward the counter in the back with a confidence that Enyo didn't feel. She sat down, placed her left forearm on the wood, and leaned forward, pinning the older man behind the counter with a look.

"Are you the village chief?" she asked.

The man before them was old but not aging. There were no wrinkles on his face. Standing tall, the tight shirt that he wore showcased his thick arms and barrel-like chest. His short hair had no gray in it, but the mustache still made him look at least somewhat distinguished.

"That would be me, I guess," he grunted, eyeing the two of them with suspicion. Enyo tried not to squirm. "What's a couple of women doing here? Travelers?"

"That's right." Fellis smiled as though she didn't feel the tension in the air. "We were hoping to get a little information, or maybe some directions to Alyssium. We're somewhat lost."

"You picked a fine place to get lost in," the man grunted.

"I've noticed," Fellis said. "It seems all of your women are missing."

"It's not a problem for outsiders to worry about," the chief said. "You mentioned wanting directions to Alyssium. It's a month's travel from here by foot and three weeks by horse. You have to pass through the Dius Mountains, which is to the west of here. You'll want to be careful, though," he warned. "There've been bandit sightings, and also, there's a rumor going around that they somehow managed to tame a really powerful monster."

Monster taming was an old profession. There were several members of the Dark Clan who excelled at taming monsters, which were then used to help bolster their ranks when they waged war. During the most recent war with Terrasole, the most popular monster to tame had been the vargr—a wolf monster that the Dark Clan used as a mount.

"We'll be sure to keep that in mind," Fellis said, and it looked like she was done talking to the man.

"Um, excuse me," Enyo spoke up. "But can I ask why there aren't any women around here?"

"I believe I said this isn't something you outsiders should worry about," the chief grunted.

"But maybe we can help," Enyo pushed. "If something has happened to them, then I'm sure Fellis and I could—"

The man slammed his hand on the table. "What could a pair of women do that we can't?! What could you possibly do that we haven't already tried?! Don't mock us by thinking you could do something that we've never succeeded at!"

Enyo was startled by the fierceness in the man's demeanor and words. However, beyond that, she felt annoyed. This man thought that she couldn't help because she was a woman? Jacob had never looked down on her for that, and the Dark Clan didn't care about stupid things like gender. It made her forget that most humans saw women as inferior.

Standing up, Enyo slammed her own hands on the table and got in the man's face. "I don't know exactly what is going on here, but don't think I'm going to put up with your rude behavior! I'm not some simpering little girl that you can force into submission by slamming your hands on the table and making a lot of noise!"

Jacob had been rude when they first met, but he'd never once disrespected her because of her gender. Even that time where he had her pretend that she was his "mistress on the side," he had stayed respectful of her position and only pushed enough to make it feel like their relationship was real. This man was just being an ass.

Wanting to make a point, Enyo unsheathed one of her daggers and stabbed it into the table between the man's fingers. "Now, you're going to tell me what's wrong, and you're going to do so right. This. Instant."

The man leaned back as she glared at him. Finally, after what felt like hours to Enyo, he sighed and gestured for her to sit back down. She frowned as she sat down, but she did not remove her dagger from the table.

"It all started several weeks ago," he began. "A few of our women went missing. We're a small town, so we noticed when they disappeared immediately. We searched high and low for them, but we never came up with anything. As the days passed, the number of disappearances increased, until all of the women had suddenly vanished. One of the farmers said they saw several women heading into a forest about a day's walk from here. We went there ourselves to try and find them, but what we found…"

The man shuddered as if he'd come down with a bad case of the chills.

"What did you find?" asked Fellis.

"All of the women had been turned into undead," the chief said.

Enyo sucked in a breath. She knew that when someone or something died, if they were not properly sanctified and cremated, they would turn into undead. However, that didn't sound like that was what happened here.

"It might be a necromancer," Fellis suggested. "Necromancy is a rare magic, but it's not unheard of for some people to have it. If there is a necromancer living in that forest, they could easily turn all of you into undead depending on how much power they have." Her brow furrowed. "That said, why would they only target just the women? It doesn't make sense."

The chief shrugged. "Your guess is as good as mine."

"Fellis," Enyo said, staring at the woman who, after a moment of looking at her, sighed.

"Do you have a room that we can spend the night in?" she asked the chief.

"I do," he said.

"How much will it cost?"

The chief closed his eyes. "This village is doomed without its women. I'll let you stay for free."

Fellis smiled. "That's fortuitous for us. After all..." she cast an amused glance at Enyo "...we don't have any money."

✳✳✳

With nothing to do but sit around and wait, Jacob decided to exercise his body. It had been put through the ringer. He was stiff everywhere; his muscles felt like they hadn't been stretched out at all, which was never a good thing for a warrior.

It had been a long time since Jacob had done any strenuous exercise. He used to train habitually, but as the years rolled by and his life had been subsumed by his role as a barkeep, exercise and training became less important. Eventually, he had stopped practicing and training altogether.

It was a wonder I've come as far as I have.

His battle with Lust made him realize something: he was out of shape. Three years ago, maybe even as little as two years ago, he would not have been defeated so easily—not by Lust, at least. That woman hadn't been as powerful as Alucard. She hadn't been the sheer destructive force that the Dark Lord had been, and yet he'd been defeated by her. It was shameful.

Jacob understood that simple exercise wasn't going to fix his problem, not fully. He could regain his former strength, but he wouldn't be able to regain the battle sense that he'd honed while traveling the world and fighting against the Dark Clan. Only experience could do that. Even so, it was a start.

He'd long since discarded his shirt. He didn't want it getting soaked in the sweat that was dripping down his back, arms, and legs. His movements were slow, his arms feeling little strain. Even though he hadn't worked out in a long time, it seemed as if two hundred push-ups still wasn't enough to call it a workout.

As he methodically continued to do push-ups, he wondered how Enyo was doing. Had she and Fellis safely escaped the city? With the battle between Lust taking up most of his attention, he hadn't been able to focus on their escape. He hoped they were okay.

They're resourceful, so I'm sure they'll be fine.

It was just as he reached his 556th push up that the doors to his room opened. He looked up as Listy walked in. She took one look at him, her eyes trailing down his back and arms, and then she frowned.

"I see you're still as uncultured as ever," she said.

"And you haven't changed a bit," Jacob sniped. "You're still a bitch."

Listy clicked her tongue. "Queen Alice is waiting for you. However, you need to take a bath before you can even think of seeing her. I'll not have someone who smells like swine come within a meter of her majesty."

Jacob thought about telling this asinine woman that he had no intention of seeing Alice. He even thought of telling her where she could shove her demand. However, that would not have been the intelligent thing to do. One doesn't ignore a summons from the queen, especially not when they were at her mercy. What's more, he had clearly been saved by Alice's knights, galling though it was to admit.

"Lead the way," he said, standing up, grabbing his shirt, and gesturing at her.

Listy huffed as she walked out of the door. "This way."

No conversation was made as he followed Listy, listening to the sound of their feet thudding against the marble floor. They had never gotten along. When he was younger, they would always argue; she would mock his attire, call him slovenly, get upset when he didn't bow to Alice or addressed her too casually, and she hated it when he and Alice had snuck off into town without her. Their arguments, for that one year he'd spent in Avant Heim, had been legendary.

It looks like nothing's changed.

Jacob wasn't given much time to wash off. Five minutes in the bath and Listy was ready to drag him out. He barely managed to get dressed before they were walking back down one of Avant Heim's many hallways.

"Where's Durandal?" Jacob asked as he looked out the window. They were passing a garden. He vaguely remembered climbing trees with Alice there, much to Listy's consternation back then.

"Your sword has been confiscated until we deem that you are not a threat," Listy answered.

Not a threat, huh? So, basically, until I break out and find Durandal myself.

Jacob had already considered breaking out, but that wasn't really feasible yet. He was strong. However, he wouldn't be able to beat the entire Terrasole army, not unless he wanted to kill everyone there, which he didn't.

Listy lead him to a large set of double doors. They were guarded by two Terrian Knights, the personal knight force tasked with protecting the crown. Stepping in front of the doors, which were ornate and covered in artful designs, Listy coughed into her hand.

"I am here to see Queen Alice. I've brought along the hero, Jacob Stone, whose presence has been requested by the queen."

The two guards shifted in obvious surprise; Jacob nearly rolled his eyes when their own widened at the sight of him. This was just another reason he despised life in the palace. If it wasn't nobles and old farts trying to butter him up—or drugging and beating him to try forcing him into compliance—then it was guards, knights, and maids gawking at him as he walked by.

Listy coughed into her hand. Startled out of their gobsmacked stupor, the guards saluted, and then opened the doors.

Trailing behind Listy, Jacob took in the familiar meeting chamber. The tiled floor sparkled, the walls were the same as always with their unique designs and the many bookcases and works of art arrayed against them. On the opposite side was a large desk. It was not the same one that he remembered. Alice must have bought a new one in the last three years.

Sitting behind the desk was Alice. Enchanting blond hair done up in elegant curls framed a face that reminded him of a fairy. Fair skin glistened in the light from the dying sun, which haloed her back, making her appearance akin to an angel's. It was often said that Alice was the fairest woman in Terrasole. He agreed. Even if he could no longer stand to be in her presence, he would never deny her beauty.

Her sense of fashion seemed to have become more refined as well, though he assumed Listy was to blame for that. Light blue with pink accents, the dress that she wore accentuated her feminine figure. It was sleeveless, exposing her arms, toned from training with a sword, yet the gloves that she wore kept her from appearing brawny. Even her bodice, which helped display her modest bust, lent itself well to showcasing her remarkable beauty.

The moment he stepped into the room, Alice's eyes had lit up. However, as he refused to smile at her, the mien of joy and happiness died down.

"Jacob, you're looking… well," Alice said, and her voice contained so many emotions that Jacob needed to clench his fists to keep from letting his own slip.

"About as well as could be expected, considering where I am."

Alice flinched. "I see… you still dislike me for what happened."

Standing up, Alice walked over to the window, pressing her hands against the glass as she looked at Jacob's reflection. It was as if he couldn't look at him directly.

"If by 'what happened,' you mean how you broke our promise, then yes, I do," Jacob said. "I don't think I've ever felt more betrayed by anyone than when you betrayed me."

"I didn't betray you," Alice said, her gloves creaking as she clenched her hands. She whirled around to face him. "I never betrayed you."

"No, you just weren't there when I needed you the most."

"I had obligations, Jacob! I still have obligations!"

"So you do. It's nice to know that you had so many obligations you couldn't even help your lover as the nobles took advantage of their position to abuse him."

"I didn't know what they were doing!" Alice defended herself. "It wasn't until you fled the capital that I even realized what they were up to!"

"And that," Jacob concluded, "was perhaps your worst crime in all this."

After several seconds of silence, Alice slowly sat down again. The look on her face, one of abject defeat, tore at Jacob's heartstrings, but he wasn't going to let her off after what she'd done, or rather, what she hadn't done. He couldn't. The nobles had drugged him, kidnapped him, tortured him, and tried to break him so he could be brainwashed, and Alice hadn't even known that he was missing from Avant Heim for an entire week. If he forgave and forgot what happened so easily, it would have been like spitting in the face of all his suffering.

Jacob closed his eyes as bitter memories surged through his mind. He could still feel the blindfold blocking his vision, the ropes digging into his skin. He could remember how the drug running through his body had affected his concentration and kept him from using Linked Energy Manipulation. More than that, the feeling of burning hot branding irons searing his skin, of flails gouging out chunks of flesh, still sometimes caused him to feel phantom pain.

"I see that talking to you won't do any good," Alice said at last.

"Glad to know we're on the same page."

Alice gritted her teeth. Behind him, Jacob heard Listy's dress ruffling. It was getting closer.

"Since you wish to be uncooperative, then I only have one question that I wish to ask you," Alice said.

"And that is?"

"Reports indicate that you have been traveling with a girl from the Dark Clan; where is she?"

Jacob smiled. "I have no idea what you're talking about. I haven't been traveling with anyone."

"One of my paladins claims to have seen you with two people." Alice glared at him. "An older woman with unusual hair and eye color, and a young girl around our age with pink eyes. Where are they?"

"The day I tell you any more secrets is the day that this world becomes consigned to oblivion," Jacob said.

"Fine," Alice whispered. "In that case, you leave me no choice. Jacob, you have been charged with treason and sentenced to life imprisonment." She signaled the guards standing at the door. They hesitated for a moment, but soon marched up on either side of him. "T... take him away."

The two guards tried to grab his arms, but Jacob yanked them out of their grip. "I can walk by myself, thanks."

Without looking back at Alice, Jacob turned around and marched out of the room. He let the two guards lead him down to the dungeon. He was amused to notice how much distance they kept from him, as if they were afraid of angering him. They also seemed hesitant. The guards were probably conflicted about sending a hero to prison.

There was a dungeon located beneath Avant Heim. Dark and cold, dank and gross, the dungeon presented such a stark contrast to the castle that it was almost funny. Mold grew along the walls. Water leaked from cracks between the stones. The cell bars were rusted and old. They cracked as one of the guards opened them.

Jacob was directed into a jail cell, which was closed and locked behind him. The two guards squirmed as if uncomfortable at what they were doing.

"We're, um, sorry about this... sir."

"Very sorry."

"It's fine." Jacob shrugged. "You two are just doing your job."

That didn't seem to reassure them, but he wasn't really concerned. Moving over to the bed, which could only loosely be defined as a bed, Jacob sat down and leaned his back against the wall. He allowed his head to slump back as he closed his eyes.

"That could have gone better," he admitted into the silence.

The silence said nothing in return.

***

Enyo lay in bed with Fellis. There was only one bed, so they had to share, but that was okay. She and Fellis had been sharing beds since she was a child.

Fellis seemed to be asleep; her breathing was even, and her chest rose and fell as she lay on her back. Enyo was wide awake. She hadn't been able to sleep. Perhaps it was because of what they were doing tomorrow, or maybe it was because she was worried about Jacob. However, her eyes refused to shut.

"Thinking about your boyfriend?" asked Fellis.

Enyo nearly squealed. After she calmed her racing heart, she tossed Fellis, whose lips had quirked into an amused expression, a glare.

"That wasn't very nice, and Jacob isn't my boyfriend."

"You mean he isn't your boyfriend yet," Fellis corrected. "It's only a matter of time before something happens. Maybe once you two are in his world, maybe sooner. He's already admitted that he likes you. That should be good enough for you to call him your boyfriend."

"Can we please talk about something else?" Enyo asked. She didn't enjoy talking about her love life, especially because she knew it would lead to this woman teasing her about how she finally had her "hero."

"Fine, then how about this: Are you sure we should be helping these people with their problem?"

Frowning, Enyo asked, "Why wouldn't we?"

"Sorry, let me rephrase that; are you sure we have enough time to spend helping these people?" Fellis didn't give her a chance to speak before continuing. "We have no idea where Jacob is, we don't know what the Dark Council is plotting, and there's a good chance that the knights are still after us. I hate to say it, but we can't afford to spend too much time helping people we've only just met."

"Speaking of the Dark Council, didn't you tell me and Jacob that they had seven champions?" asked Enyo. "To the best of my knowledge, we only fought six."

"Given that Lust showed up on her own, I am beginning to suspect she did not have a champion," Fellis said. "I never learned who she chose, so I just assumed she was being secretive. Now stop avoiding my question. Do you really think we have time to help these people?"

Enyo was silent for a moment. It wasn't because she didn't have an answer, but rather, she was trying to figure out the best words to express herself.

"Do you remember when I was younger and would constantly tell you that I was going to marry the hero one day?"

A fond smile lit Fellis's face. "How could I forget? You were like that even before Jacob had been summoned to this world."

Feeling the heat creeping across her face, Enyo continued. "A-anyway, when I first decided to marry the hero, it wasn't because I wanted to marry him, but because heroes are legendary figures who save people. Throughout history, heroes are the ones who go on adventures, fight evil, and rescue people from tyranny. When I said I would marry the hero, it was because I wanted to be one of those legendary figures who rescued others."

Enyo raised her hand and looked at the ceiling visible between her fingers. She could make out strange lines and patterns along the worn-out wood.

"This is my chance to be a hero like Jacob is," Enyo continued. "So far, all I've done is follow Jacob as we journey. We've helped a few people here and there, but we haven't done anything truly heroic, but I have the chance to do that right now. I'm not going to let it slip by."

Maybe it was selfish of her, to want something like this when there was so much at stake. However, Enyo didn't want to deny herself this chance.

"What about Jacob?" Fellis asked.

"There's no way Jacob is in trouble," Enyo said, full of confidence. "He's stronger than anyone else I know. He beat my father, who was hailed as the strongest Dark Lord to have been born in the last five hundred years. Someone like him would never be killed off by anything or anyone."

"Heh? You have such amazing confidence in your boyfriend— sorry, I meant your future husband."

In the face of her former maid's words and teasing smile, Enyo could do nothing but hide beneath the covers.

"Shut up," she mumbled, trying to ignore the heat surging through her cheeks.

She wasn't very successful.

***

It was early in the morning when Enyo and Fellis set out. Using the directions given to them by the village chief, they wandered across a vast grassland, toward the forest where all the women of the village had disappeared into.

The area they were in was actually a valley, Enyo had learned. When she and Fellis had been swept away by the river at the bottom of that ravine, it had taken them to this valley set between several hills and mountains. It was an isolated area, which explained why none of the men had recognized her.

There hadn't been a single wanted poster in that village.

As they crested a hill, a large mass of trees came into view, spanning out for what appeared to be several dozen kilometers. Giant trees twelve to twenty times taller than her loomed in the distance. It wasn't even close to the Phantasma Forest, but having grown up in the darklands, it still felt large to her.

"That must be the forest that the necromancer is hiding out in," Fellis said.

"Are we sure it's a necromancer?" asked Enyo. "There are other things it could be."

"Such as?"

"A serial killer who killed all the women but never properly cremated them."

"I hope that's not the case. It'll make our job a lot harder."

Enyo conceded her former servant's point. If it was a serial killer, then it meant all of the women weren't brought back via dark magic, but the curse. If it was the curse, then it also meant they would need to find and kill each undead. However, if it was a necromancer, then all they needed to do was kill the one who brought them back. They could also allow the villagers to properly cremate their loved ones, provided they had a priest capable of sanctifying the corpses.

The trees were a lot larger than Enyo had first realized. There might not have been as much mileage here as there had been in the Phantasma Forest, but the trees were far larger. They were massive, towering over her like giants. Roots jutted from the ground, each one larger than she was, creating a twisting network that reminded her of a maze. She'd never seen anything quite like it.

"Well," Fellis said, patting her whip. "Let's head inside. The village chief said there are supposed to be ruins in the center of this forest. That's supposedly where most of the women have been seen."

"We should still keep our guard up," Enyo said. "There's no telling where those women might be. If they are being controlled by a necromancer, then there's a chance we could be ambushed."

To be on the safe side, Enyo unsheathed her daggers as they wandered into the forest. She was immediately assaulted by the sounds of forest life. Birds cawed, crickets chirped, and the sound of rustling and growls echoed all around her. The forest floor was littered with twigs and leaves, which crunched underneath their feet.

"This place… is really creepy," Enyo muttered.

"You're the one who wanted to come here."

"I know that! And I wouldn't have changed my mind even after knowing this. I was just saying that it's creepy."

"This place is enough to give someone the chills, I agree."

Enyo was thankful to Fellis for talking to her. It helped ease the tension she felt. Her shoulders became more relaxed, and her muscles felt more limber, which was good, as she needed to remain loose and flexible to get the most out of her body.

A new sound alerted her to the presence of something else; the sound reminded her of something being dragged along the ground.

"Fellis?"

"I hear it. Something is coming."

She appeared from around one of the large roots. It was a woman with glossy black hair and a thicker than average body. Her arms were strong and her legs had a lot of muscle. She must have been someone who had spent her whole life working in the fields.

Lumps had formed on pallid skin, and spots had appeared in her eyes, which had become entirely white and milky.

"This is an undead?" Enyo asked, repulsed.

"Yep." Fellis pulled out her whip. "Get ready. There are two more behind her."

Indeed, with the woman were two other women wandering toward them. Enyo only had a moment to be shocked. Then the woman in front, followed by the women in back, lunged at her and Fellis.

Enyo leapt back and put some distance between them. At the same time, she channeled dark magic into her daggers. As they were infused with dark black flames, she lashed out, sending a dark energy blade at the first woman. It cut into the female's flesh. Coagulated blood sprayed across the ground. This didn't stop the woman, who lunged at Enyo again.

"Aim for their heads!" Fellie said as she wrapped her whip around one of the undead's necks and pulled. There was a sickening popping out. The head came off with a disgusting amount of ease, as if the woman's body had been decomposed so much it could no longer hold itself together. Thick, black blood oozed from the severed stump. The body slowly fell to the ground.

Enyo, wanting to end this quickly, channeled more dark magic into her blade. She swung it at the first woman. A large black crescent like Jacob's attack was launched from her blade. It slashed into the woman's neck, which split apart like an overripe fruit. As her head left her shoulders, the woman crumpled to the ground, and there she remained.

There was only one more woman to take care of. Enyo spun around to face her last foe—only to see that Fellis already had the undead well in hand. A flick of her wrist and the whip shot out. The tip slashed into the undead's throat, tearing it apart. Enyo thought she could actually hear the sound of the undead's bones being cracked. It looked like the whip had even severed her spinal column. With her head barely attached to her shoulders, the woman, a young female with long blonde hair, fell backwards with a dull thud.

"Let's keep going," Fellis said.

"Yeah..." Enyo stared forlornly at the women they'd been forced to kill. "We should hurry up and free these women, so they can rest in peace."

Fellis placed a hand on Enyo's shoulder. "Are you sure you're up for this? You know that we might be forced to fight more undead."

"I know... I still want to help. Even if it's just freeing these women from the shackles of Aemon's Curse, I want to do something for them."

"I understand." Fellis removed her hand and gestured for Enyo, who followed her as they left the scene of the battle. "At least now we know that they're being controlled by a necromancer. That attack was way too coordinated to be a couple of regular undead."

Enyo nodded, but she didn't say anything. With a sigh, Fellis took the lead as they trekked through the forest. The two of them wandered around, over, and under roots, and journeyed through organic tunnels made of wood. There were no more attacks, which Enyo was grateful for. It was her hope that she and Fellis could kill the necromancer without having to kill any more of the women.

One of the many "root tunnels" that they traveled through eventually opened up to reveal a cliff. It was only a short drop. Down below was what appeared to be the remnants to an ancient civilization. It wasn't a village, however, but a maze with a large wall that would keep most people from being able to climb it. In the center of the maze was a building made of old, tan stone. Enyo thought it looked like a temple.

"I guess this is our destination," she said.

"Probably," Fellis replied. "I doubt there are many other places like this located inside of this forest."

"Then let's go. I won't let whoever's controlling these women remain in control any longer."

Climbing down from the ledge was not difficult. The vines along the cliff face allowed her and Fellis to scale down to the bottom.

With the maze now before them, Enyo felt a strange sense of apprehension. She couldn't quite put her finger on it. However, dread welled up in the pit of her stomach, like if she stepped into that maze, she would never come back out.

"This will be our last chance to turn back," Fellis warned. "Are you sure you want to do this?"

Enyo squared her shoulders. "I'm sure."

"Okay." Fellis let out a slow breath, and Enyo realized that she was nervous, too. "Then let's go before I can change my own mind."

Screwing up their courage, she and Fellis traveled through the entrance. Their feet tapped against a stone floor instead of gravel. The passage they walked through was pretty wide. If they were ambushed, Enyo felt confident that she and Fellis would have enough room to maneuver around in. Even so, she hoped they didn't end up engaged in combat with those undead.

As if life was trying to screw with her, upon turning the next corner, they ran into several undead. No, not several undead—at least one hundred undead. Milky white eyes stared at them. Although those eyes were blank, emotionless, Enyo thought she found a primal hunger burning within them.

"Enyo?"

"Yes?"

"I think we should run."

"I agree."

Enyo and Fellis spun around and ran back the way they'd come. The undead lunged after them, scrambling over each other as if eager to taste their flesh. They burst around the corner like a horde and chased after the two of them with the ravenousness of starving trolls.

Her heart pounded in her chest as they turned a corner, only to find more undead coming from the other direction. She and Fellis turned down the only lateral passage there. They raced down the enclosed space, which branched off into several more directions that they were forced to choose at random. Sweat had broken out on her forehead. Raspy breathing escaped her parted lips. It wasn't from exertion, but from the exhilaration of having her life placed in jeopardy. The simple joy she felt at being placed in a situation that could kill her caused some bloodlust to rise up within her, though this feeling also made her feel guilty.

"F-Fellis…" she gasped, feeling her mind cloud over. She wanted to fight. She wanted to feel the ecstasy of battle, to bask in the blood of her enemies.

"This way," Fellis said, grabbing Enyo by the forearm and pulling her along.

They went into another lateral passage, which branched out several more times. There didn't seem to be any rhyme or reason to the makeup of this maze. Enyo couldn't even comprehend why it had been created in the first place.

It was getting harder for her to breath. She could feel her mind slipping into a haze of bloodlust. Enyo tried to fight it, tried to ignore it, tried to push it to the back of her head, to lock it away where it wouldn't make her do something she'd regret. She couldn't. The harder she tried, the stronger her bloodlust became, until it was an overwhelming force fueled by the side of her that she hated the most.

Turning another corner, she and Fellis ran into a dead end. Fellis cursed. Enyo smiled.

"Damn it! Now we're trapped!"

"It's fine."

"W-what?" Fellis looked her way. "E-Enyo?"

"Don't worry. I can deal with them."

The smile on Enyo's face widened as she turned to face the incoming horde. Undead filled the passage. They were like a tidal wave of decomposing bodies.

"Attero. Consumo. Erado. Perimo. Vasto. Extinguo."

There was a strong tug on her navel as magic was pulled from her to power the spell. It traveled through body, flowed up her back and down her arm, and was unleashed from the palm of her hand—a massive wave of dark fire. It surged across the passage, consuming everything in its sight. The undead were annihilated, the walls were incinerated, the floor disappeared. Nothing could withstand it. When the attack ended, all that remained was a massive trench that must have been at least a kilometer long.

Her attack complete, Enyo came to. She was horrified.

"Oh…" She held a hand to her mouth. "I… I can't believe… I did it again…"

"Enyo…" Fellis started, only to trail off, as if unsure of what to say.

"Why? Why can't I control my bloodlust like you can? Fellis… why am I so different?"

Fellis hesitated for a moment. "I suppose it's because of your heritage. You might have been sired by the Dark Lord, but do not forget that you also have a mother."

Her mother. Enyo had never met the woman who'd given birth to her, not for any reason like she'd been abandoned or something, but because her mother was dead. When she was old enough to understand, she'd been told that her mom had died at childbirth.

"Your mother was a human, which is who you received your light magic from," Fellis continued. "Being half human means you are unable to fully control your bloodlust like most members of the Dark Clan."

The fact that her mom had been a human was a secret. To the best of her knowledge, her father had even gone out of his way to keep this information from the Dark Council. In fact, the only person who she believed knew about this was Fellis, and that was because Fellis had been her mother's lady-in-waiting before becoming Enyo's maid.

"It's times like these that make me wish I'd been born fully human," Enyo muttered.

Bloodlust was a powerful driving force among the Dark Clan, and Alucard, being the Dark Lord, had a particularly strong bloodlust, which Enyo had inherited. Thanks to that, every moment that she was locked in combat was a struggle against herself. The Dark Clan part of her loved fighting, loved battle and violence and killing. The human part hated it and everything about it. This duality was another reason she wanted to travel to Jacob's world. Maybe if she lived in another world, one where she didn't have to fight, her struggle could finally be put to rest.

"Come on, Enyo." Fellis placed a hand on her shoulder. "Let's put an end to this by finding that necromancer and making him regret what he did to these women."

"Yeah… you're right."

Standing up, Enyo regained her bearings, screwed up her emotions, and followed Fellis. With pretty much all the undead—or at least most of them—having been destroyed, it was easier to reach the temple.

Now that she was up close, Enyo could definitely say it was a temple. The walls were made of large stone blocks. Massive and worn, with cracks spreading along much of the structure, the temple showed its age. Honestly, it was a miracle the thing was still standing.

They walked past numerous evenly spaced columns. A flight of stairs marked the entrance. There was no door, just a large open space. She and Fellis walked right in.

Darkness. Everything aside from the entrance was cast in shadow. She could barely see a meter in front of her.

"Lux."

Creating a ball of light with a simple incantation, Enyo illuminated the room. It looked like a great hall. As she and Fellis walked further in, their footsteps echoing ominously, she showered light in multiple directions to take in the scene. The walls were all painted with murals. She couldn't quite tell what the murals were about, but they featured what she guessed were humans and dragons. The humans were all on the ground, kneeling as if in prayer. The dragons were devouring the humans.

That's not a very pretty picture.

At the end of the hall sat a dais. A broken chair that might have been a thrown at one time, but was now a derelict piece of stone, was the only remnant to suggest this place belonged to someone important. Enyo imagined people coming to this place, perhaps to worship the dragons in those murals. Perhaps the one who sat in that chair had been a priest or a king.

"Enyo, shine some light behind that throne."

Doing as instructed, Enyo directed the light to illuminate a portion of the wall. There was a large door. She imagined that the door had once been a magnificent piece of architecture, but now it was just like everything else. Faded. Aging. It looked like it was made of bronze, but it was covered in rust and stains. She wondered if it would even open.

"Do you think you can slice through that with your magic?" Fellis asked.

Enyo bit her lip. "Maybe."

She walked up to the door. Pressing her hands against it, she studied it, though she didn't know what she was looking for. In the end, all she could do was attempt to slice through the door with her magic.

Should I use light magic or dark magic?

Dark magic was excellent when it came to destroying things, but it was also indiscriminate. Even blades created from darkness had a bad habit of destroying more than necessary. Light magic, the offensive kind, was great for precision work, but she didn't know if it would pack enough power to slice through this door.

Let's try light magic first.

If light magic proved ineffective, she'd go with dark magic. That said, she really hoped the light magic would work. Enyo didn't want to use her dark magic right now.

"Lumen. Lamina. Segmentum."

Enyo felt the tug on her navel. She held out her hand. Light coalesced, gathering particles of photonic energy soon became a single, solid entity. Then it took shape. A handle formed within her hand. The blade thinned, becoming sharp. Forming on the end was a tip, while the area above her hand became a crossguard.

Enyo didn't really use swords because she'd been trained with daggers, but daggers probably wouldn't have been thick enough to cut through this door. Enyo took a deep breath. She slid her feet along the ground, bending her knees. Bringing the sword up to her face, she thrust it forward, impaling the door.

She met with resistance. Gritting her teeth, she shoved further, further, until her blade was buried all the way to the hilt. Then she brought the blade down. Her arms shook, muscles strained. Enyo wasn't that strong physically. Her style relied on stabbing weak points or enhancing her dagger's cutting power with magic. While magic was being used here, this door seemed to be obnoxiously resistant to her light sword.

After what felt like hours, Enyo finally managed to cut a misshapen hole through the door. She wiped the sweat from her brow and sighed.

"Ugh, that was way harder than it should have been."

"Think of it this way." Fellis smiled as she walked past her. "At least you were able to give your magic a good workout."

"Work out, my butt," Enyo muttered. She was exhausted. Even her bones felt brittle from having expended so much energy.

The interior was dark, but with Enyo's light to guide them, they were able to see that the next area was a tunnel. The walls were even more dilapidated here. Cracks spread along every inch—except for the places where entire chunks of the wall were missing. Likewise, the floor was broken, and the fragments made some places unstable to walk on. Enyo almost fell when her foot smacked a section of the floor that had been upturned.

"I wonder what kind of place this used to be?" she pondered out loud.

"Well, it's obviously a temple," Fellis said. "I imagine this was a place where the draconians used to live."

Draconians were a rare species of half-human, half-dragon hybrids. They'd been created by the Dark Lord Catus in the war two thousand years ago. No one knew if the draconians were still alive. According to the few records in her former home, they had very low birth rates due to their longevity. Draconians could live for around one thousand years. They might have died out by now.

There was another door at the end of the hall, though this one was already demolished. Stepping through, Enyo and Fellis were greeted by a foul stench and a strange light that came from the center of the room. There was a magic circle in the room. It glowed brightly, though its color was dark—a deep purple that emitted a vile sensation. Just being in the room with it made her skin crawl.

There was a person standing in the center of that circle. Cloaked from head to toe in darkness, she could see nothing about them beyond the curve of their chin and the twist of their lips. They were pale, but it wasn't the kind of natural paleness like members of the Dark Clan possessed. It was more like a chalky, never-goes-outside sort of pale.

"What's this? Guests?" The man, for that voice could have only been a man, tilted his head. "How odd. I didn't expect to have any guests so soon. I don't even have food prepared for you."

"You're a necromancer, right?" Fellis asked, stepping forward. "I'm guessing you're the one who murdered all those women?"

"Murdered? Me? Murdered? No, sorry. I don't murder people. The only thing I do is grant them new life."

Enyo clutched her daggers more tightly. "Turning them into undead isn't granting them new life! It's turning innocent people into abominations!"

The man sighed. "You clearly understand nothing. Ignorance like that is unbecoming from people like you. I can tell from your magic and appearance that you're both members of the Dark Clan. Surely two from the clan of darkness can recognize my work for what it is."

"The only thing I recognize is that you murdered those poor women to satisfy your twisted desires," Enyo snarled.

"Don't bother talking to him, Enyo," Fellis declared. "This man isn't going to listen to reason. He's clearly lost his mind."

"What a cruel thing to say," the man said. "I don't much appreciate being insulted by my guests. Still, I suppose it is my lucky day. I was just about to do an experiment, and you two will make excellent guinea pigs."

The magic circle lit up even more. Enyo was blinded by the brightness. Forced to close her eyes, she raised a hand to shield herself further from the light, only lowering her hand when the light died down.

Two new people were standing in the room, though they didn't appear to be all there. One was female and the other male. Their well-muscled bodies flickered several times, as if they were fragile illusions. Scales covered their hands all the way up to their biceps, and long claws emerged from their fingers. They wore no shoes, but like their hands, their feet were scaly and clawed. Expressionless eyes gazed at her and Fellis.

"It seems my experiment was a success," the man crowed. "Yes! After all these years of research, I've finally managed to summon draconians from beyond the grave!"

"This… doesn't look good," Enyo muttered.

Fellis sighed. "I'm beginning to regret letting you bring us here."

Enyo was given no chance to retort, for the man, his lips pulled back into a depraved grin, pointed at them. "Go, my draconians. Slay these two foul creatures! Show them that my experiment is a success."

The two draconians bent their knees. Enyo and Fellis tensed, but Enyo was dealing with more problems than her former maid. Her heart rate was picking up. She could feel her body growing warmer at the thought of combat. Blood surged through her veins as everything seemed to slow down.

Then the draconians blasted off the ground so fast that she could barely see them. Enyo yelped as she dove out of the way. Behind her, a loud rumble nearly burst her eardrums. She turned her head. The door that she had entered through was gone, as was most of the wall.

S-so much power!

Several meters to her right, Fellis was already engaged in combat with the female draconian, and it looked like she was having trouble. Unlike the male, the female fought more methodically. She'd charged until she was right in front of Fellis. Then she slashed out with her claws. It was dodged, Fellis contorting her body like she was boneless. Most attacks were narrowly avoided but a few weren't. Some slashed through her clothes, and a line of blood flew through the air when the draconian drew a thin cut along her torso.

Enyo was no longer able to pay any attention to her former servant's fight. The male draconian had emerged from the hole he'd made, and he was charging right at her again. He moved so fast, too. She barely had time to prepare before he was attacking her with his clawed hands. Unlike Fellis, who relied on dodging and contorting her body to avoid damage, Enyo used her daggers to deflect the attacks.

It proved harder than she'd imaged.

An overhead strike was blocked. Enyo thought her arms would snap like brittle twigs. When the draconian came in next with a series of vicious attacks, she moved backwards, angling her raised blades so each blow glanced off. Even with this, however, every attack sent her stumbling back. The strength of this draconian was so far above hers it wasn't even funny.

The only thing that might hurt this creature is magic.

Unfortunately, she didn't have time to cast a spell. Attacking her with a vicious claw thrust, the draconian nearly impaled her, but she swerved away at the last second. Even so, she could feel the air being cut.

I need to get some distance.

Backpedaling to avoid another swipe, Enyo didn't even see the tail coming until it was already plowing into her stomach. She saw, more than felt, her body as it flew through the air. Everything passed by in a blur. The world spun. Then her mind was overridden with pain as she slammed into the ground.

"Enyo!" a shout came from somewhere in the distance. It sounded familiar, but Enyo couldn't recall who it belonged to.

Blinking several times, Enyo tried everything she could to clear the cobwebs out of her head. It wasn't until she saw a shadow looming over her that she remembered where she was.

Enyo rolled along the ground. A tail smashed into where she'd been laying, pulverizing the stone floor. She felt her eyes go wide when she saw the dent left by the tail.

If that had hit me—

Enyo wasn't even able to complete her thought before the draconian turned to her. Scrambling to her feet, she rushed down the hall. She needed to somehow even the playing field. Behind her, the draconian roared, and the stomping of feet caused the ground to shake.

The hallway was long. She felt like she'd been running forever. The sounds of the draconian's mad stomping and roars were getting closer. Enyo peeled her lips back and bared her teeth as she darted across the last few meters of space in the hallway. She rushed through the hole she'd made in the door, dashed past the dais, and then spun around and prepared to cast a spell.

She needn't have bothered.

The draconian male hadn't made it to where she was. He'd stopped halfway between the throne and the door, prowling back and forth as he snarled at her. She frowned. Why had he stopped chasing her? Why was he just walking back and forth? He'd been so intent on ripping her limb from limb that she was sure he'd have been eager to pounce the moment she stopped...

... Unless he can't move past a certain point!

There was a lot that she didn't know about necromancy, but she did know that it followed a set of rules. One of them was that the more powerful a creature was, the less distance it could traverse from the one who reanimated it. Like a tether attached to an animal, it couldn't travel any further than a certain distance from its master.

Enyo didn't hesitate to begin chanting.

"Purgo. Procuro. Purifico. Perputo. Perpurigo. Purgatio."

There was a massive tug on her navel as a good portion of her magic was drained from her body. Light emitted from her palms, coalescing into a bright golden orb that crackled in the center of her hands. Her legs shook. Her arms wavered. Yet she remained strong as massive amounts of energy gathered around her, until the orb had grown to four times the size of her head.

Then the orb shrank to barely two centimeters in diameter.

Then the orb was fired.

Enyo expected many things. With an orb that could travel at the speed of light, she expected it to slam into the draconian, send him flying back, and then turn him into dust as his body was purified. What she didn't expect was for the draconian to swat her attack away. As the orb crashed into a pillar, demolishing it, Enyo struggled to keep her jaw from becoming unhinged.

That... is just so not fair!

So even one of her strongest light spells wouldn't work against this thing? How could she beat something that her spells couldn't injure and her blade couldn't... cut...?

... Wait a second...

As another plan formed in her mind, Enyo unsheathed her daggers and charged at the draconian. What she was about to do was dumb. It was the dumbest thing she'd ever done—dumber even than running away, stealing the gate key while it was in route to Avant Heim, and traveling across Terrasole in search of Jacob.

It was also the only thing she could think of.

The draconian didn't get the chance to attack first. She struck before it could, thrusting the dagger in her left hand at its chest.

"Purgo."

Light emitted from the dagger, and the draconian's scales sizzled. Even if it wasn't human, it was still an undead, and thus it had the same weakness to light magic that all undead had.

"Procuro."

It tried to attack her, but Enyo was prepared, having gotten a read on its movements thanks to their last few bouts. She dodged its claw swipe, leapt over its tail, and then stabbed it in the exact same spot with her other dagger. Its scales began to melt.

"Purifico."

The draconian howled as it attacked with more ferocity. Enyo wove between a hailstorm of slashing claws, making sure to use the fact that the draconian couldn't move past the throne to her advantage. She moved back, avoided a swipe, and then came back in. Stab. Blood poured from the wound as her dagger finally pierced his scales.

"Perputo."

Another dodge. Another stab. The wound became deeper.

"Perpurigo."

By now, the draconian seemed to realize that something was wrong. She was injuring him. He went into a frenzy, attacking with a series of furious slashes. She merely moved past the throne, came back in, and stabbed him again. Blood gushed from the wound.

"Purgatio."

On her last attack, Enyo thrust her dagger into his chest with all the strength she possessed. The weapon slid in, piercing his chest as, with her final incantation, she poured all of the magic she had left into this one attack. The results staggered even her.

Cracks appeared along the draconian's body. Beams of light shot from his eyes. His body shook as the cracks widened and spread.

Enyo leapt back just as the draconian exploded into millions of light particles. She raised her arm to shield her eyes, and when the light dimmed, she lowered her arm and looked at the place where the draconian had been. He wasn't there anymore.

I... beat him?

It took a moment for that fact to sink in. When it did, she raised a hand to her mouth, as if trying to contain the squeal that wanted to emerge. She couldn't believe that she had defeated a draconian—and without using her dark magic to boot!

After taking a moment to congratulate herself, Enyo remembered that Fellis was still fighting in the next chamber over. She rushed back into the hall and down the corridor. The other room soon opened before her.

Fellis was still fighting. Her body was covered in bruises and lacerations. Blood ran freely down her skin. Meanwhile, the draconian looked like she was in perfect shape.

As a woman and someone who used a whip, Fellis was at a distinct disadvantage when fighting against another female, especially one that was this strong. Her whip was practically useless against those tough scales. What's more, half of her fighting style relied on using Mind Manipulation to control someone and make them present openings in their guard. However, it was hard to use Mind Manipulation on a woman while in the middle of combat, since Fellis couldn't seduce women. Would Mind Manipulation even work on an undead anyway?

Enyo could have gone over to help her former maid. Perhaps if they double teamed the draconian, they could win. However, Enyo knew of another way to win, one that had a lot less risk.

The best method to kill the puppet was too get rid of its puppeteer.

"That's right! Murder that bitch! Kill her! Rip her to shreds so I can free her from these bonds of life!" Like a lunatic, the necromancer's laughter rang with the overflowing twang of insanity. He hadn't even noticed her yet, busy as he was goading the female draconian on.

Enyo didn't want him to notice her approaching, so instead of getting in close and attacking, she hung back, channeled light magic into the dagger in her left hand, took aim, and threw it. Her aim was true. The dagger soared through the air and pierced the necromancer through the skull. His laughter stopped immediately. He remained standing for several seconds. Then his body began to twitch before he fell backwards with a boneless thud.

The draconian, with no one providing her magic, began to evaporate. Before she fully disappeared, she smiled at Enyo, as if giving thanks for freeing her from the necromancer's control.

"Enyo!" Fellis rushed to her side. "Are you all right? Are you hurt anywhere?"

"I'm fine," Enyo said. "I'm really sore, but I think I'm in better shape than you are."

Fellis paused, then sighed, and then smiled. "Yes, I suppose you are correct. You did quite well." She sighed again when Enyo muttered a healing spell that took care of her injuries. "Thanks."

"You're welcome," Enyo said. "Now, I think we should get out of here. I don't know about you, but I don't want to be in this place anymore."

"That," Fellis started, "is a grand idea."

***

The villagers had been grateful when Enyo and Fellis returned that day and let them know that the necromancer had been destroyed and their sisters, wives, and children had been put to rest. The villagers let them stay for the night. When morning came, they provided the pair with food and saw them off.

"Thank you for all your help," the village chief said. "And… I'm sorry for thinking you weren't capable of helping us. I'm glad you proved me wrong."

Enyo smiled sadly and shook her head. "You're welcome. I only wish we could have done more for your families."

While Enyo had taken the villager's thanks with a smile and some kind words, Fellis had stood back. Enyo thought it was because, unlike her, her former servant didn't care to become a hero.

When all was said and done, she and Fellis said farewell and left the village. Following the directions given to them by the chief, they traveled to the west, toward the Dius Mountains. Their goal was the Daedalus Pass, a route through the mountains that would take them to Alyssium.

The Dius Mountains was a massive mountain range. The tallest peaks were so high they seemed to pierce the heavens. Enyo couldn't even see the tops, shielded as they were by clouds.

As they walked through the Daedalus Pass, which took them between mountains, Enyo glanced at the cliff faces that stood on either side of them. There weren't many places to climb. However, there were a lot of ledges that could have been used as ambush points. The village chief had warned them about bandits in the area, so she wanted to be careful and therefore kept a constant surveillance of their surroundings.

"Do you know how long it'll take to reach Alyssium once we pass through these mountains?" asked Enyo.

Fellis hummed. "The village chief said it would take a day to travel through Daedalus Pass without interruption. Once we pass through the mountains, it will take another twenty-nine days to reach Alyssium. As long as we don't run into trouble and keep to a strict pace, it should take exactly one month."

Enyo tried not to let her depression show. She'd been hoping they could shave that time off, but if even Fellis was telling her it would take a month, then she had no choice but to concede.

Daedalus Pass was a winding path that traveled up, down, and around the mountains. She and Fellis were sometimes forced to climb up steep cliffs and travel through dark tunnels to keep going. No one ambushed them as they walked, there were no monsters coming out to "greet them," and Enyo believed they could pass through the mountains without incident.

Hindsight is always 20/20.

It happened when she and Fellis were about to cross a bridge. Several men leapt down from the ledges on either side. They were a ragtag bunch; their clothes were threadbare and in tatters, they were missing teeth, and their skin was covered in filth. Rusty weapons were clutched in grimy hands. Sweat-covered faces stared at her and Fellis with obvious lust in their eyes.

Enyo felt dirty from those looks alone.

She didn't bother letting them speak. Before they could even open their mouths, her daggers were out, and she was charging at them. She killed the first bandit without any of them doing a thing, stabbing him through the heart and slitting his throat at the same time to make sure he died swiftly. Enyo wasn't going to cry over one less bandit in the world.

"W-what the fuck, Lady?! You just killed Ezio!"

"Of course I did! You think I'm going to let you get a word in when I already know what you're here for?" Enyo shouted as she rushed at next bandit.

He swung his blade, a rusty falchion, at her, but she deflected it with the dagger in her left hand, and then thrust out the dagger in her right. Her weapon pierced his chest. He was dead before he hit the ground.

"You could at least listen to what we have to say!" the bandit, who she assumed was the leader, shouted.

She scoffed. "Right. Because I don't already know what you're going to say: 'You have to pay the toll if you want to cross the bridge.' Then once we've given you everything you own, you'd take us prisoner anyway so you could turn us into your playthings. I know how this works, but I have a tight schedule to keep and no desire to play around!"

Two bandits tried to double team her, one wielding a claymore and the other a short sword. Enyo winced a little as her left dagger clanged against the massive claymore. Ignoring the small jolt that traveled through her arm, she redirected the weapon into the other bandit's path, moving her arm up, over her head, and around to the other side of her body. Even she winced when the claymore dug into the man's skull, killing him instantly, though that didn't stop her from slitting the claymore wielder's throat.

"Well said, Enyo," Fellis agreed as she wrapped her whip around one of the bandit's necks. She yanked him off his feet and threw him into one of his comrades. As they both went down, the one on bottom accidentally pierced that one that she'd thrown through the chest, killing him.

"Damn it!" the bandit leader swore as Enyo rushed forward and attacked another bandit. "Who the hell are these broads?! Shit! I guess we got no choice! Bring out Echidna!"

"Echidna?" Enyo asked.

Above them, a man with a black robe and a hood stood on a ledge. Enyo blinked when she noticed the tunnel next to him, which explained how they had ambushed her and Fellis without being spotted. She didn't have much time to contemplate the man as he ran into the tunnel. Another bandit was trading blows with her. Fortunately, he was about as skilled as most bandits were.

That is to say he had no real skill to speak of.

Enyo wove around his reckless and imprecise swings, feeling the air currents shift during each attack. This man's sense of timing was atrocious. Once she'd gotten a feel for his attack patterns, she lunged forward, swerved around his awkward swing, kicked out his legs when he attempted to backpedal, and then sliced his clavicle vein as she ran past his falling form. She heard him hit the ground behind her.

Now she had a clear shot to their leader. Even though she tried not to, Enyo couldn't quite stifle her grin when she saw the horror-stricken expression on the man's face. Her blood was boiling. She wanted to kill this man, this filthy creature who was beneath her contempt, who murdered and pillaged and raped. She wanted to—

Enyo's instincts warned her of danger, screaming at her and making her leap backward. Something crashed into the ground in front of her. A person. No, a monster. She had the upper half of a woman. A sensual figure was bared for all to see. The curve of her neck was slender and elegant. Her face would have been beautiful were it not for the way her mouth split open to show off a gaping maw full of sharp teeth.

As the woman bared her ugly mouth at Enyo in a snarl, she peeled her lips and proceeded to snarl right back—until she noticed the woman's lower half... which was that of a snake.

"S... sn..."

"Uh oh," Fellis muttered as she tore through a man's throat with the steel tip of her whip. "Enyo, remain calm. Don't panic and—"

"SNAAAAAKKKKKEEEEE!!!!!"

Enyo's scream echoed across Daedalus Pass. Memories from when she was a little girl flooded her mind, unpleasant at best and terrifying at worst. They were memories of scales and fangs and

biting and poison. There were few things in this world that she really hated. Injustice was one of those things. Snakes were another.

A red haze fell over Enyo's mind as her thoughts were subsumed by the terrible memories from a time of her childhood that she'd rather forget. She could remember nothing of what happened in those few seconds. When she finally came to, Fellis was shaking her shoulder and calling her name.

"Enyo! Enyo! You have to calm down! The echidna is already dead so calm down!"

"What? Dead?" Enyo blinked, and then she blinked again. Then she looked down. Lying at her feet, with black fire covering its body, was the echidna. "When did that happen?"

"That happened when you went berserk and killed it," Fellis said.

"I killed it?"

"Yes, you did—along with all the bandits that were around here."

"Huh." Enyo scratched the back of her head as she took note of the bandit corpses lying all around her. "I don't remember doing anything of that."

"That's because you went crazy." Fellis placed a hand on her forehead and sighed. "Honestly, Enyo, losing your cool like that in the middle of combat is unbefitting of a warrior."

"B-but snakes are frightening," Enyo said. "You know I don't like them."

"Yes, yes. I know. Ever since you were bitten by a venomous snake when you were younger, you've always hated them. I am aware. I was the one who made you the antidote, after all. However, you should have mastered this fear a long time ago."

Enyo looked away. She didn't want Fellis to see her blush. "I-it can't be helped. It's not like I've seen that many snakes since then, and this one also had the body of a woman. It was double creepy."

Fellis had never looked so exhausted. "Let's just go. I'd like to arrive at the next village before midnight."

The two crossed the bridge and continued traveling, leaving behind several dead bandits and the burnt remains of an echidna.

INTERLUDE I - COUNCIL DECISIONS

Lust was the youngest member of the Dark Council, having killed the previous Lust in single combat several centuries ago. The previous Lust, along with the previous Pride, had been the oldest members before their deaths at her hands. While the current Pride may have spat vitriol at her due to the "dishonorable" way she had killed his old man, no one else really cared, and they often sided with her over him.

That said, she didn't really care about the council. They were just a means to an end. She was only there to be amused.

In short, they were her playthings.

"Lust," Pride said, his voice full of scorn. "Is it true that you fought against the hero?"

"I did indeed," Lust admitted. "It was quite the battle. I can see how he was able to defeat Alucard. Our champions were no match for him either."

The Dark Council never did realize she didn't send a champion of her own. If they asked, she could just inform them she was her own champion.

Pride's scornful look tickled Lust's insides. "Praising the hero, Lust? I hadn't realized you could lower yourself any further, but it appears I was mistaken. Where is your pride as a member of the Dark Council?"

"I'm sure you have enough pride for the both of us." Lust smiled. "I'm Lust, in case you've forgotten."

"If you fought the hero, then does that mean you also found the Dark Lady?" Wrath asked, his voice a deep baritone filled with anger.

"Sadly not," Lust said. "It appears the Dark Lady had already escaped before I faced off against the hero."

Pride scoffed. "Not only do you have no pride, it seems you're useless as well."

"Coming from a man who can do nothing but bitch and whine, those words mean very little to me." As Pride gave her a look filled with hate, Lust addressed the rest of the council. "While I was not able to capture the Dark Lady and bring her back, I did manage to discover where she is traveling."

"And where is she traveling?" asked Sloth.

"She is heading to Alyssium," Lust announced, nearly giggling when an unsettling stillness hung in the air.

"Why would she travel to Alyssium?"

"If she goes there, all of our plans will be ruined!"

"What should we do?"

Listening to these old codgers panic was like music to her ears. These fools, powerful beyond compare, were little more than deranged schemers who'd long since lost their claws. They had lived for too long, become too comfortable with their status quo.

She would not become like these idiots, and she had a plan that would bring this boring standstill that they had been locked in with the White Council to a stop.

"If I may," Lust began, once more gathering everyone's attention. "I would like to propose that we attack Alyssium."

Silence reigned once more. She could sense the incredulity in her contemporaries's gazes. They probably thought her mad, and maybe she was a little out of her mind, but it was better to be insane and happy than sane and bored.

"You want us to attack Alyssium? The stronghold of the White Council?" Wrath asked, and for once, the anger was not there. Lust thought he was contemplative more than anything.

"Of course, we will not be going to challenge the White Council," Lust added, lying through her teeth. "Our ultimate objective is to reclaim the Dark Lady. With her no longer in our sights, all we can do is travel to Alyssum and wait for her to appear."

"You are a fool," Pride spat. "Starting a war with the White Council will accomplish nothing. We are too evenly matched."

"Now where is your pride?" Lust asked with a mocking grin.

"My pride has been tempered by experience, whelp! I have lived through countless wars! You don't survive the battlefield like I have by being stupid! There is a difference between being prideful and being arrogant!"

Pride was always so easy to rile up. Say the littlest thing, give the slightest insult, and he flew off his hinges. She loved his amusing reactions. It made screwing with him all the more fun.

"While your idea has merit, I have to agree with Pride on this matter," Envy said. She was the only other woman on the council. Lust didn't know much about Envy, who kept to herself. Lust assumed she was the reclusive and cautious type.

Subjugating her might be difficult, but it would be oh-so-fun too.

"In that case, why not allow me to go and acquire the Dark Lady for us?" Lust offered.

Pride looked ready to shout her down, but Wrath beat him to it. "How do you plan to reclaim the Dark Lady?"

"It's simple. I'll infiltrate Alyssium and lie in wait. When the Dark Lady finally arrives, I will capture her before anyone can realize that she is there."

The council conferred, which basically meant they shouted to be heard over everyone else, who were also shouting. Lust didn't partake in their idiotic form of debate. She never did. Instead, she listened as they argued over her plan, combed through it as if they could somehow discover a flaw within it—or, in the case of Pride, tried to deny her this mission because it would hurt his—well, his pride. She took it all in, hiding her smile behind a haughty veneer.

In the end, they could not justify a reason to not let her go.

"We believe this is the best choice to reclaim the Dark Lady," Wrath said. "Therefore, we shall let you travel to Alyssium. However, because you fought the hero and nearly blew our cover, you will not be going alone. Pride will go along with you."

So, the oldest fart of them all is coming with me? That's fine. This will give me the perfect chance to exterminate him.

"If that is this esteemed council's wish, then it shall be so." Lust smiled at Pride. "I look forward to working with you."

"And I'll be keeping my eye on you to make sure you don't screw up again."

"Of course."

The black figures, thought-transmitted images, vanished one by one until only Lust was left. She gazed around the council room, envisioning how magnificent this place would be if it became her private throne room. Given time, she was sure she could make that vision a reality. Everything was going according to her design.

She was leading the council around by the nose, and they didn't even know it.

***

Lust met up with Pride a day after the council decision, and the two of them soon set off on their journey together.

It was rather uneventful.

"Oh, my! Look at how beautiful this necklace is! Do you think it would look good on me?"

"Why the hell are you asking me?! Can't you just shut up?! And stop attracting so much attention to yourself! What are you?! A whore?!"

"Well, someone is in a grumpy mood."

They were wandering through a small town, which Lust did not know the name of. It was located in Terrasole and was about 10 days travel from the darklands.

As Lust placed the necklace she had been admiring down, Pride scowled at her. His aged face made her think of dried parchment. Meanwhile, his rail-thin body, which appeared to have been made of twigs, was clad in a dark cloak. Bright silver hair jutted from his head at odd angles. His pink eyes created an odd contrast to the rest of his face. Like all dark clansmen, he had pointy ears, but they were currently hidden beneath his hair.

"Every town we visit, you always go off and begin shopping. What is wrong with you? Can you not show at least a modicum of refinement? You act like a barbarian."

"Better to act like a barbarian and have fun than a stuffy old man whose claws have been clipped," Lust replied with a shrug.

Pride's scowl became even more fierce.

They eventually found an inn at which to spend the night. Attached to the inn was a simple pub that only served a few items, like flaked meat pies and beef stew with curds and whey.

Lust spent most of her time flirting with the young waitress who, despite telling Lust that she was not into women, still ended up falling prey to her clutches. That was the thing about youngsters. It didn't always matter if they were heterosexual or not. Beauty was beauty, and Lust was rather prideful of her looks. She was confident in her ability to seduce even straight women.

"You are disgusting." Pride curled his upper lip as he sat in the stiff wooden chair.

"And you are a gross old man," Lust shot back as she leaned in her chair like it was a throne, thrusting out her chest and grinning as several men from across the table eyed her.

Dinner wasn't what Lust would call fantastic, but it wasn't bad either. She ordered a stew with roasted pig belly. As she ate her food, she smiled at Pride as the man sniffed the food several times.

"Checking for poison?" she asked.

"I don't know how humans can eat this garbage." Pride's scowl was something to behold as he ate placed the cut of beef in his mouth. "It isn't even cooked right."

Lust said nothing and simply enjoyed the meal, pretending to be heedless of Pride's suspicious stare.

The next day, the two of them set off again. Pride had come into her bedroom and nearly choked to death when the man saw the young barmaid and several other men lying naked in her bed. He'd scolded her something fierce, but Lust only smiled, which seemed to infuriate the man further.

Two more days passed before Lust decided it was finally time to make her move. Pride had been keeping a suspicious eye on her for the longest time. However, even he could not be on guard constantly. That time came when they were traveling down a deserted highway that stretched out for several kilometers in either direction.

Pride was walking ahead of her, his eyes staring straight ahead as if he was trying to ignore her. She produced a dagger from her sleeve and wandered behind him. Before he knew what was happening, she thrust her dagger into his back.

Or that's what should have happened.

Before Lust knew what was happening, her body slammed into the ground as something pressed down on her. It was as if the world had suddenly been dropped onto her shoulders. She gritted her teeth and struggled to look up.

Pride sneered at her. "Did you really think I did not know what you were up to? The others might have been fooled, but I've known all along that you're nothing but a traitorous rank whore who does not care for the ideals of the Dark Council. It seems biding my time and waiting has finally paid off. Now I can kill you and the council will not be able to say a thing."

Lust struggled to stand up, but it was nearly impossible with so much weight pressing against her.

"So… this is… Suppression Magic? H-how frightening."

Suppression was the name of Pride's magic. It was simple in concept but complex in how it worked. His magic basically allowed him to suppress all living things. She'd never seen his magic at work before, so she hadn't known what to expect, but it definitely lived up to its reputation.

"I wonder what I should do with you?" Pride said with a grin as he walked around her, secure in the fact that she was unable to fight back. "Given how you murdered my father, I definitely need to take some form of revenge before killing you. I even thought of raping you, but then I realized you would probably enjoy it. So then… what shall I do?"

"How about you… let me go?" asked Lust. "Haven't you ever heard the saying 'forgive and forget'?"

Lust tried to push herself to her feet, but the moment she made the attempt, the ground beneath her cracked as the weight on her shoulders increased even more. Her face slammed into the ground. She released a pained groan as blood welled up inside of her mouth.

"Ha ha. You are a funny one." Pride's laugh was dry. "However, there is no forgiveness with me. Hmph. I suppose I should just kill you. Then I can string your naked corpse to a horse and have it run across the kingdom. That will be a fitting punishment for someone like—hurk!"

Pride's words were abruptly cut off when he stumbled. He placed a hand against his mouth and coughed several times, falling to a knee. When he removed his hand, it came away stained with blood.

"What…?"

"There are quite a few poisons in this world, and not all of them need to be consumed," Lust said as the man started coughing again. More blood spilled from his mouth, splattering against the ground as she stood up and grinned at him. "There are poisons that can infect people through skin contact, airborne poisons, and of course poisons you can put in food. I like the airborne poisons myself. Quite a few of them are odorless, tasteless, and you don't have to apply it manually. Just let someone breathe it in. The only problem is, they take a few days to work their way through a person's bloodstream."

"So you… you poisoned me…? How? I didn't see you… release—hack!—release any poison into the air!"

"You do know what my magic is, right? Oh. I suppose you don't. You never did learn how my magic works even after I killed your old man." Lust giggled as she mocked the man. "A pity."

"Bitch…"

"Thank you for the compliment."

Pride tried to speak, but he was no longer able to. Blood spewed from his mouth the more time passed. Lust watched with a grin as his legs and arms weakened, as he fell onto his face, and as his body began twitching. After he stopped, she tapped his forehead with her toes.

"Are you finally dead?" she asked. She received no response. "Good riddance."

With a tap of her foot, Lust created a large hole beneath Pride's corpse, and then closed the hole back up after he fell in. With a soft hum, she continued on her way. It was unlikely that anyone would find out about what happened here.

CHAPTER 2 - ALYSSIUM

It took a month and a half to reach Alyssium. They probably could have gotten there sooner if they'd gone straight from the village to there, but Enyo had wanted to help several people along the way. Fellis might have been upset, but Enyo thought it was obvious. Heroes helped people. What's more, if Jacob had been with them, he would have helped these people. Since he wasn't there to do it, she'd do it in his stead.

Getting into Alyssium was surprisingly easy; all they had to do was dye Enyo's hair again. She also changed her eye color using light magic to bend the light around her eyes. It took effort to maintain, but she was pleased to say that no one recognized her.

They had also changed their outfits.

Fellis was now wearing black pants that hugged her frame, a long-sleeved white shirt with a tan vest and a black trench coat thrown over it. She had complained about not being sexy enough, but Enyo thought her sexiness was the problem. The woman invited too much attention.

Alyssium was not quite what she had pictured it to be. Walking along the paved roads, turning her head left and right, Enyo took in the sights and wondered where all those rumors of golden buildings and jewel paved roads had come from. Certainly, Alyssium was beautiful, with its well-maintained roads, aesthetically appealing houses made of brick and tiles, and the many smiling faces of its citizens. However, it wasn't anything special.

As they walked through the street, stall vendors called out to potential customers, saying, "Buy our amazing products for a limited time bargain." Stores showcased their latest wares in windows. The scintillating scent of delicious food wafted from food stalls. On any other occasion, Enyo would have loved to explore the place.

But this wasn't just any occasion.

"Here we are," Fellis said. "Alyssium. It's a lot smaller than I expected the capital of Terrasole to be."

Indeed, while it was a truly massive city, it wasn't gargantuan like Tallus Caelum had been. Surrounded by a large wall, built into what seemed like several tiers with Avant Heim in the center of it all, Alyssium appeared no larger than Altus or Albany.

"Let's find a place to gather information," Enyo suggested. "I want to find out if there's been any sightings of Jacob."

"Do you really think Jacob will be here?" Fellis asked. "I don't mean to be rude, but he was fighting against Lust. She's a member of the Dark Council, one of the people who control the Dark Lords from the shadows, and is not to be underestimated."

"Jacob is fine," Enyo said. "I don't care who that lady is. There's no way he would lose to anyone—and you can laugh and tease me about having confidence in my future husband all you want. Go ahead. I dare you."

"Tch!"

For the past month and a half, Enyo had been subjected to Fellis's teasing. Whenever Jacob was brought up, Fellis would say something to try and invoke a reaction from her—and it worked more often than not, but Enyo was catching on. She wasn't going to let Fellis's teasing affect her anymore.

Their first step for gathering information was to find a good bar. However, bars didn't have a lot of patrons until later at night, and it was midday right now. That meant they had time to get a feel for the city.

Enyo spent that time well, wandering the city with Fellis, pretending to be a tourist who was visiting from a small village several days away. Just like she'd expected, Alyssium was built into three tiers. The bottom tier was the market and lower-class district, the middle was the residential district where the wealthy lived, and the upper tier was the location of Avant Heim, which was surrounded by another gate.

Walking into what appeared to be a village square, Enyo was drawn to a large crowd of individuals who stood around a man standing on a platform—a teller. It looked like he was going to announce something important.

"I wonder what they're going to talk about," Fellis said.

"Let's find out," Enyo decided.

Walking into the crowd, she and Fellis listened to the teller as he read from a sheet of parchment. "Hear ye! Hear ye! The one known as Jacob Stone, the Hero of Terrasole and Slayer of the Dark Lord Alucard, has been arrested for treason."

A shockwave rippled through the crowd. Whispers broke out. People began talking in hushed voices that grew louder over time, until a threnody of loud shouting echoed across the plaza. Enyo barely heard any of it. She was in shock.

Jacob was arrested? What?

"He was traveling alongside the thief who stole an important treasure from the royal family, and he has fought against our paladins many times since joining up with this thief. Jacob Stone has become a traitor to the crown and the people of Terrasole. Thus, he has been sentenced to life imprisonment."

Enyo felt like someone had just clenched her heart in an ironclad grip. Meanwhile, the many conversations around her gained coherency.

"Jacob is a traitor? Impossible!"

"How could our hero be a traitor?"

"What do you mean? Don't you remember how he abandoned us?"

"That's right! He disappeared when we needed him the most!"

"I bet you he was conspiring with the thief to steal from the royal family all along!"

"There's no way that can be true! Jacob saved my parents and I during the invasion!"

"He's a traitor!"

"He's innocent!"

A line soon formed, a division between the people. One side remained steadfastly on Jacob's side, but the other side, which slowly grew as it gained more fervor, believed what the teller was saying. That side, fueled by anger, began to shout down the other side. As the people, clouded by an unusual rage that felt unnatural, became angrier by the second, Enyo felt more and more like she was drowning in a sea of negativity.

"Come on," Fellis said, and the sound of her former servant's voice and the feeling of a hand grabbing her own snapped Enyo out of her fugue. Fellis pulled her along. They left the plaza, journeying further away until the voices vanished.

Enyo was still in shock. She couldn't get those enraged voices out of her mind. Were humans really like this? That anger, that rage, that vitriol—it had almost felt like they were members of the Dark Clan suffering from bloodlust. Beyond that, however, there was…

"I can't believe Jacob was arrested," she mumbled. "How did this happen? When did this happen?"

"We're not going to find that out by idling around," Fellis said. "Let's find a place to stay, and then we can work on gathering information about what happened."

Enyo nodded. "You're right. Of course you're right. Let's do that."

Going off in search of an inn, Enyo's thoughts went out to Jacob. She hoped he was okay.

INTERLUDE II - A QUEEN'S ANGER

Alice stormed down the hall of a largely unused section of the castle. This area, which consisted of giant arched hallways and living spaces reserved for guests of the crown, only had a few people present— seven, to be exact. This place, Avant Heim's west wing, was where the White Council resided.

Behind Alice, Listy walked on silent feet.

The White Council was the advisory council of the royal family; it was their job to disseminate information gathered from across Terrasole, report it to the king or queen, and advise them on the best actions to take.

For many centuries, this method had worked fine. However, ever since Alice had taken up the crown, a division had appeared between her and the White Council.

When the White Council gathered, it was always within the private meeting room located in the west wing. Alice reached the doors, behind which the White Council sat right this instant. Two guards noticed her approach and saluted.

"Your Majesty!" they announced.

"Open the doors," Alice said without pause.

Upon hearing the order spoken with such an authoritative voice, the guards could do nothing but obey. They pulled on the handles and opened the double doors. Alice stormed in.

She glanced around the room. White walls with golden murals depicted Terrasole's glorious history. A domed ceiling was painted to look like a clear blue sky. There was a round table in the center of this room, and sitting around it were the seven members of the White Council.

Alice did not know their names. The White Council, upon accepting the position, took up one of seven names based on their virtue. Most of them were old men with wrinkled skin and wizened appearances, but one of them was a young man with black hair, and the other, a young woman whose bronzed skin gave her an exotic look.

"Your Majesty," one of the older men said as he stood up. "We were not expecting you. Is something the matter?"

"Yes, something is the matter," Alice said through gritted teeth. "Who gave you permission to let everyone know about what happened with Jacob? And do not lie to me and say that you have no idea what's going on. I was informed just a moment ago that several tellers were wandering around Alyssium with parchments bearing the royal seal."

Despite her words, no one there seemed surprised. Indeed, from their calm expressions, it almost seemed like they'd been expecting her reaction. The thought made her frown.

The youngest among them stood up. "I apologize, Your Majesty, but I was the one who sent the notice out to inform the public."

"Chastity." Alice narrowed her eyes. "What right do you think you have to go over my head on this matter?"

"Correct me if I'm wrong, Your Majesty, but I was under the belief that the law dictates that when something of vital importance to the kingdom happens, the people are to be notified immediately."

"Yes, but only when it is of vital importance," Alice stated. "While the... betrayal of Jacob is indeed a serious matter, it does not affect the citizens. What's more, it is not you who decides what the citizens are and aren't allowed to know. That is the monarch's obligation and duty. That you not only made the public aware but also went over my head on this matter is every bit as grave as what Jacob did. Should I perhaps inform the citizens that you are a traitor trying to use his position to usurp the crown?"

Chastity twitched as a vein appeared on his forehead. "Your Majesty, while what I did was in error, I felt at the time that you were in an unfavorable situation. We all know that you and the hero were once close. Imprisoning him must have been difficult. It had been my hope to alleviate your burden by—"

"Your job is not to alleviate my burdens," Alice cut off. "It is to give me council so that I might make the best choice for my people."

She knew what Chastity was trying to do by appealing to her emotions. He was attempting to make her believe that his only desire had been to alleviate the stress placed on her by the crown, that he was being understanding of her position. Alice knew the truth. He was attempting to undermine her authority.

It had long been known to her that many of the White Council members were against a female monarch. There hadn't been a queen without a king for five hundred years, and that queen had nearly brought their nation to ruin when a dark clansman infiltrated the kingdom's government. It had taken two hundred and seventy-eight years for their nation to recover. Since then, the idea of a queen ruling had become a frightening prospect for them.

From the time she'd become queen to now, the White Council had done everything they could to undermine her authority. It was mostly small matters, a comment here that questioned one of her decisions, a remark there about how her father would have made a different choice regarding one policy or another. They sought to make her lose confidence. However, through thick and thin, and even after Jacob had disappeared, she had refused to bow down to their whims. It was the reason she and the White Council clashed regularly.

She watched carefully as Chastity attempted to control his emotions. His hands were clenched, knuckles white and arms shaking. He took several deep breaths, as if to keep from lashing out, and then he settled down…

… and smiled.

"Yes, you are right. Of course, Your Majesty," he said at last. "I will accept full responsibility for what happened."

"Hold on there, youngster," one of the older men said. "There is no need for this matter to get out of hand. Alice—"

"Your Majesty," Alice corrected. "Please refer to me by my proper title, Justice."

Justice was an old man—the oldest one on the White Council. At nearly ninety-four years of age, he was almost ready to kick the bucket. His face, lined with wrinkles, sagged in several places. He sat with a noticeable stoop and walked with a cane, making most people mistake him for a feeble old man. Alice wasn't fooled. Justice was not only the leader of the White Council, but the most powerful sorcerer on the council.

"My apologies, Your Majesty," Justice replied easily, as if he was not bothered by the testiness in her tone. "It is sometimes hard not to remember when you were a young ball of energy and refer to you as such."

So he was trying to play the grandfather card, was he? He hadn't brought that one out in a while. However, she could play this game just as well.

"I do not think it's that hard, considering it has been over ten years since you last called me Alice," she said, smiling. "Refrain from doing so again."

"Of course, Your Majesty," he said, bowing to her.

"I will only give you all this one warning," Alice continued, addressing everyone this time. "None of you are in a position where you can make decisions that affect the people of this country. Your roles are advisory ones and nothing more. If any of you goes over my head like Chastity did, I will send you to stay with Jacob—and since Chastity has set the precedence, everyone in Terrasole will know by the marrow. I hope I have made myself clear."

She received a round of affirmatives from everyone, though in the case of Kindness—the female—all she got was a nod. It was good enough, for now.

Seeing that her point had been made, she left the room and began walking down to a different section of the castle, one far removed from the castle proper.

"It looks like Chastity is bolder than the others," Listy said now that they were no longer near the White Council.

"He is certainly foolish," Alice determined. "Did that man truly think I would not see through his ruse? He might have gained a council seat due to his skills as a magician, but he's clearly lacking as a politician." She glanced at Listy out of the corner of her eye. "I want you to keep an eye on that man."

While there was no evidence to suggest that something was afoot, Alice's instincts were warning her about Chastity. She did not like the aura that surrounded him.

"I will make sure to tail him when he leaves after the council meeting," Listy promised.

"Thank you."

Exiting a door that lead to a courtyard, Alice walked through a wonderful garden with an array of colors. It was like a sea of multi-colored blooms. Flowers of many types spread their petals, releasing a soothing aroma that calmed her mind. She always loved walking through the gardens. It reminded her of when she and Jacob had played hide and seek there.

She and Listy reached a tower. The guard standing watch saluted as he opened the door.

"Please wait here, Listy. I won't be long."

"Yes, Your Majesty. I will wait here."

Alice smiled when she spotted the look on her friend's face. Listy did not approve of how she was going down to see their prisoner, not that she didn't understand why. Still, her maid said nothing, and for that, Alice was grateful.

She walked down a flight of circular stairs, entered another room, and looked at the guards. There were two. Both sat at a long table, playing what appeared to be a game of cards. She coughed into her hand.

"Ah… Your Majesty," one of the guards stuttered. Both stood up and saluted.

"Has there been any word from the prisoner?" she asked.

"No." The guard shook his head. "We've learned nothing. He barely even speaks to us."

"I see." She sighed. "Then perhaps I can get him to speak. Carry on with your game."

The two guards turned red, but she was already traveling through the jail cell, stopping only when she reached the cell that had one particular prisoner.

Jacob looked the same as always. He wasn't wearing a shirt, and his body was covered in sweat, showing that he'd been exercising a little while before she'd come in. She took a moment to admire the way his abs flexed as he shifted around to get comfortable, fondly remembering a time when she had licked sweat off those abs…

She shook her head. Now was not the time.

"How have you been, Jacob?" she asked softly.

Jacob looked at her, then looked away and grunted. "The food sucks, I don't get to take baths, and my guards keep trying to interrogate me. Other than that, I'm fine."

"Perhaps if you stopped being so stubborn and told us where your companion is, they wouldn't interrogate you so much."

"You know me; stubbornness is in my nature. Is there some reason you're here, or were you hoping to interrogate me as well?"

"You know I would not interrogate you. I… merely wanted to see how you were doing."

"In that case, since you have now seen how I'm doing, why don't you go ahead and leave?"

Alice closed her eyes as if doing so would somehow block out the pain. His words hurt more than he knew—or perhaps he was saying them because he knew they would hurt.

"I remember a time when you and I used to be close. What happened to those times? Do you really hate me this much?" she asked.

Years ago, before Jacob had even entered the war against the dark clansmen and Alucard, back when he was still being trained, she and Jacob had been thicker than thieves. They'd done everything together. They had even slept together—well, they had tried. Her father had put a stop to that when he realized she'd been sneaking out of bed to sleep with him.

Even after the war, they had been close. In fact, they had been even closer after the war had ended. Alice could still recall the feel of his hands on her, of his strong arms as they wrapped around her waist, of his shoulder as he let her rest against it, of fire and passion and his body as they bared themselves to each other. Those days had been some of the happiest she'd had.

"I don't hate you," Jacob sighed.

Alice was startled. "E-excuse me?"

"I have never once hated you," Jacob said. "I do not hate you. I don't think I could even if I tried."

"T-then why have you treated me like this?"

"Because I've come to realize something." Jacob finally stood up from his small bed. Looking at her with his eyes that reminded her of a clear sky, he gave her a frown that shook her down to her core. "You and I live in different worlds. What we were, what we tried to be, it can never happen. I'll not go down a road that will leave me picking up the pieces of my broken life again. You've already broken me once, Alice. I'm not the type who'll allow himself to be shattered twice."

Alice felt an acute pain in her chest, like a thousand hot needles poking her heart. Jacob was basically saying that their relationship had been a fool's errand from the beginning, that everything they'd done had been meaningless. What made the situation worse was that she could not refute him. They had tried, they had done their best, but in the end, her duty had consumed her life, and she'd left Jacob to fend for himself.

"I... yes, you are right," Alice said at last. "I guess... we really are different."

Yes, they were a lot different. Jacob would not have abandoned her had their positions been reversed, but then, he was also not a monarch. He was a man who lived by the beat of his heart. She was a woman who lived in the cage known as royalty, with all the responsibilities, obligations, and trappings that came with it. They came from different worlds.

"For what it's worth, I am sorry," Alice continued. "I never meant to abandon you."

"I know." Jacob's smile, unlike the last one he'd given her, was reassuring. It made her feel even more awful than if he'd spat at her. "I think that makes it worse."

"I suppose it does," Alice said, and then she left.

She didn't want Jacob or anyone else to see her tears.

***

It was later at night. The meeting between the White Council had just ended. Chastity had left with the others, though unlike them, his destination was not the residential district but the market district.

While it was known as the market district, it didn't have just vendors, stalls, and shops. The market district was also home to taverns and inns. Chastity's destination was one particular tavern with a faded old sign that said *Hero's Stop*.

It was, in all regards, an average tavern. Fairy lamps hung from the ceiling, the warm wood panels and inviting atmosphere lent itself well to the establishment. Numerous patrons sat around tables or in booths, while barmaids wandered around taking orders and doing their best to avoid harassment. The sound of chairs sliding along the ground was barely heard over the obnoxious singing from a couple of men who'd had a little too much to drink.

Chastity found an empty booth and slid in. While he waited for his acquaintance to arrive, he ordered an ale from the barmaid, subtly flirting with her by complimenting her eyes and hair. From the way the girl blushed, Chastity knew that he'd be getting some tonight. This was only confirmed when she came back and slid her address to him along with his ale.

"My, aren't you popular," a voice said as a cloaked figure slid into his booth. Chastity could see nothing of her face save the gentle curve of her jawline and her lush ruby lips.

"Are you jealous?" he asked.

The figure's laugh was like tinkling wind chimes. "Hardly. I have more than enough men waiting on me hand and foot. I'm merely stating that I understand how you feel."

"Is that so?"

Chastity wouldn't deny that he was a little disappointed. He hadn't seen this woman without her hood up, but from what little he'd managed to glimpse, she was a woman of extraordinary beauty.

"How was the meeting with the White Council?" asked the woman.

"It was the same as always," Chastity grunted. "Just a bunch of stuffy old men whose time in this world has long since passed. The only bright spot in that council is Kindness, but she never speaks and so I've been unable to properly get her in my bed."

The figure nodded along with him. "I understand the feeling. As one of only two girls on my council, I often have to deal with arrogant old codgers as well." She paused. "Tell me, did the queen come in and put a stop to what you were doing?"

"She did." Chastity scowled when he remembered the queen's pompous reprimand. "I don't understand why those old men put up with that bitch. She has no good qualities. She's arrogant and stiff. That woman needs to get laid."

"Are you sure that's not just your own perception of things?" asked the cloaked woman. "It sounds to me like this woman does a good job of keeping people in line."

"You're taking her side?!"

"Am I not supposed to? Shouldn't we women stick together?"

It was difficult to determine if this person was making fun of him or not. Damn it. He really wished he could see her face. It would have made determining her personality much easier.

"So, the events at the meeting played out as I expected," the cloaked figure said, tapping her index finger against the table. "That's good. It means my predictions of her were accurate. This will make predicting her in the future that much easier."

"If you say so." Chastity glanced around the room, listening into some of the nearest conversation. "It looks like everyone is talking about Jacob Stone becoming a traitor."

"Speaking of, you mentioned that Jacob is being held in a prison located within Avant Heim."

"That's right. The queen is keeping him inside of the castle dungeon, lord knows why. I guess she wanted to keep her toy around to have fun with him."

"You say that like it's a bad thing," the cloaked figure said.

Chastity stiffened when something rubbed against his crotch, causing blood to well up inside of him. It took him a moment to realize it was the woman's foot.

"Do you not enjoy being played with?"

"I… I don't mind being played with," Chastity admitted. "But I prefer to do the playing."

"Oh, my. Perhaps once this is all over, I'll let you play with me. How does that sound?"

Chastity took a shuddering breath, trying his best not to become too aroused, or let this woman know about it, at least. He couldn't afford to let her have the upper hand. He needed to be in control at all times.

"I certainly wouldn't object. However, if and when this happens, it will be done on my terms."

"Of course."

Perhaps it was the way her lips curled, but Chastity had the strangest feeling that he was playing into this woman's hands. The thought bothered him. However, it was just a strange feeling that he had, so he pushed it aside.

"You mentioned before that you can help cement my power base," he said to get them back on track.

They had been speaking for nearly two weeks now. She'd been a huge help in getting him recognized enough to be granted the honor of becoming a White Council member. The other council member had died of an illness. He suspected that this woman was somehow involved, but he had no proof, and in the end, he didn't care. It was because the previous Chastity had died that he rose to this position.

"I did," she conceded. "However, before we get into that, I think we should get rid of your watcher."

"My what?" Chastity blinked.

The woman smiled. "You mean you didn't know? Someone has been watching you this entire time." Chastity panicked. He was about to look around, but the foot on his crotch suddenly pressed painfully into him. "Ah ah ah. Don't look. If you look, you'll give away that we know about her."

"W-what are we going to do?" asked Chastity.

"You leave that to me," she said as her lips curled into a cruel smile.

Chastity had never seen something more beautiful, or more terrifying, in his entire life.

He offered up a silent prayer for whoever was spying on him.

CHAPTER 3 - POLITICAL DEALINGS

It was late in the evening when Enyo and Fellis decided to gather information. They'd chosen a bar that had more traffic than most, with numerous patrons coming into and out of it, sitting at tables, and just making as much noise as possible. She and Fellis sat at the bar. Fellis had bought an ale. Enyo thought about getting something to drink so that she'd look more natural, but she didn't want to drink unless required. She still remembered the horrid taste of alcohol from the last time.

She also remembered how drunk she'd gotten.

Several eyes were on her and Fellis; she could feel them, like nails raking against her skin. They made her feel dirty, but she put up with it. They were there to gather information. She needed to find out where Jacob was being held.

This particular bar served a lot of knights. They were easy to recognize, and not just because many of them were still in their armor. Those who didn't wear armor carried weapons.

She'd learned early in their walk through Alyssium that the average citizen was not allowed to carry swords, perhaps because this place was the capital, so there should have been no need for weapons. Enyo didn't understand, but she was of the Dark Clan. Everyone, even children of the Dark Clan, carried weapons.

Enyo was eyeing one knight in particular, a very familiar paladin with dark hair and dark eyes. It was the man who Jacob had run into back in Tallus Caelum, the same man who chased her in Altus. She also suspected that he was the one who arrested Jacob.

"Good evening, ladies," a voice said. "I couldn't help but notice that you two were alone, and I thought it was a crime that such lovely young flowers had no one to share their evening with."

Enyo turned. The person who'd spoken was a handsome young man with the air of an aristocrat. His defined features were handsome, but not overly so. Jacob was more handsome than him. He wore refined clothes befitting a noble, silk pants and a crimson doublet.

"Can I help you?" asked Enyo.

"Indeed you can," the man said with a gracious smile, "by allowing me to buy you a drink."

Enyo debated the merits of letting this man buy her a drink. She wasn't a fan of alcohol, but she knew that if she wanted to get information, then she needed to present a harmless and vulnerable front. She needed to play up to this man's ego and loosen his tongue. At the same time, she really, really, *really* did not want to get drunk.

I wonder if I could use magic to keep myself sober?

She'd never tried it before, but it was worth a shot.

Enyo muttered under her breath.

"Protego. Vocatus."

"Excuse me?" the noble questioned.

"It's nothing," Enyo said with a smile and a shake of her head. "Please sit down."

Despite not being well versed in flirting, Enyo did her best to entertain the noble, whose name she didn't even care to know. She basically tuned out everything he said, smiled, and nodded. He didn't seem to care anyway. From what she gathered, this man liked listening to the sound of his own voice.

Time dragged on as she listened. It was easy to not pay attention and still achieve positive results, since the man seemed to be paying more attention to himself than to her. Also, her spell was working quite well. She'd already finished one mug of ale and wasn't feeling anything. The ale still tasted awful, though.

Out of the corner of her eye, Enyo saw Fellis entertaining several men. She felt envious at how naturally her former maid spoke. Unlike her, Fellis didn't appear to have any trouble playing the flirting game.

"... And recently, my father has been trying to free my brother-in-law from prison. I honestly cannot fathom why he would do such a thing."

"Speaking of prison," Enyo started now that she'd seen an opening, "is it true that the hero has been sentenced to life imprisonment for betraying the crown?"

Well and truly drunk, the man thought nothing of nodding as he said, "So it would seem. I know someone who works in the palace as a guard, and it appears that the hero is locked up in the dungeon."

The dungeon...

"The dungeon is in the palace?" she asked.

"Of course," the noble said. "All criminals captured in Alyssium are sent there until they can be transported to Cocytus. Didn't you know that?"

"I'm not from around here," Enyo said as she eyed Fellis, who was now playing drinking games with three burly men. Two of the men were already passed out on the floor, and the last swayed drunkenly in his chair. She looked at the man's red face as he blinked several times. Fellis, on the other hand, still looked completely sober as she smiled at the man.

She shook her head.

"Anyway, thank you for being so kind as to speak with me. However, I really must be going now," Enyo said.

"W-what? Going?" The noble's eyes widened. "But we've only just—"

"Fellis, let's go," Enyo said as she stood up.

Fellis looked at her, and then back at the man sitting across from her. She flicked the man on the nose. That seemed to be all he needed to fall back and pass out on the floor. Bounding to her feet with a satisfied grin, Fellis gestured for her to lead the way.

They exited the bar and disappeared into the street. Enyo glanced up at the sky, dark velvet and shining with stars. The bar they'd gone to didn't second as an inn. They would need to find a place to sleep.

"I take it you got what you needed?" Fellis asked when there was no one else around.

"Yes," Enyo said. "I know where they're keeping Jacob."

"What's our next course of action?"

"Not here. Let's talk about that once we find a room for the night."

They were about to continue walking off—when Enyo felt something that made her stop. The hairs on her neck were prickling; goosebumps had appeared on her skin. She felt a strange chill in her bones. This feeling, what was it?

"Someone is using dark magic," Fellis said.

"Can you feel it?" Enyo asked.

"I can."

"Can you track it?"

"Possibly."

"Then please do what you can."

While Fellis might have desired to say something along the lines of, *"We can't afford to waste time protecting people we don't know,"* she seemed to have realized that Enyo wouldn't listen. She didn't even hesitate to do as asked. She glanced around, her ears twitching as if they could hear something beyond Enyo's ability to perceive.

"This way," she said before running off.

Enyo followed Fellis into an alley. They burst out the other side, only to travel through another alley. Fairy lights blurred past her vision; colors seemed to meld. Enyo wondered where they were going, but then she saw it—there was someone on the roof, and they were being chased by strange monsters!

"Those are wraiths!" Fellis said.

Enyo didn't respond. She chanted instead.

"Penitro. Percutio. Perfringo."

Enyo felt a tug on her navel. Light coalesced before her hand, streamers that gathered and formed a blade, which shot forward so fast it appeared to have teleported. The light spear pierced one of the monsters, a strange wraithlike creature made of black shadows.

Shrieking, the creature stumbled and fell off the roof, hitting the ground and shattering like glass.

Two of the monsters stopped chasing the woman, turned around, and leapt at her and Fellis. They avoided the pounce by splitting apart. Enyo chanted again, feeling the familiar pull on her magic as she sent a light spear at the beast. It dodged. She clicked her tongue.

"Close quarters it is," she muttered.

Fellis was already engaged in combat with one of the wraiths. She danced around the creature, chipping away at it with her whip. Enyo would've marveled at how graceful the woman was, but she had her own problem to deal with.

Unsheathing her daggers, Enyo channeled light magic into her weapons, causing them to glow a brilliant white. The wraith charged forward, but she swung her weapons forward. Her foe reared back as she sliced into its flesh. It hissed, steam wafting from the wound before it closed up.

"Your kind is weak against light magic," she said, grinning.

The wraith didn't understand her words. They were not intelligent creatures, merely violent ones. All they could do was attack or follow the orders of something or someone stronger than them.

This one attacked her again, its previous wariness forgotten. It lunged at her once more, but Enyo stepped to the side, allowing it to pass, and then she brought her daggers down and pierced the creature's back. As light energy erupted from her blades, it burned the wraith's body from the inside out. The monster evaporated into the night.

Fellis was still fighting her wraith. Her magic made her ill-suited to battling creatures like this, which were little more than dark matter given form. The woman wove around the various attacks sent her way. She ducked a claw swipe that ruffled her hair, leapt away from a swing that would have torn open her chest, and then struck the creature with her whip. Sadly, physical attacks didn't work on monsters like this unless enhanced by Magic Channeling.

Knowing this, Enyo threw a dagger at the wraith, which pierced its back while it was busy defending against Fellis. The creature shrieked as light emitted from inside of it. Then it burst into light particles.

"That was excellent work," Fellis complimented. "You did a good job."

"Thank you," Enyo said. "Do you think that girl is all right?"

"I am fine," said the very girl they spoke of. She walked out of the shadows, revealing herself to the two of them, though to say that she revealed herself would be an oxymoron. She was wearing a dark cloak that hid everything, including her face. "Thank you for the assistance. Because of you two, I was able to defeat the last wraith without worrying about counterattacks."

"You're welcome." Enyo smiled. "But why were those wraiths attacking you anyway? What were they even doing here?"

"It is odd that a couple of wraiths would be found in Alyssium," Fellis added. "The only way for them to get inside here was if someone had summoned them."

"I'm afraid that is exactly what happened," the woman said. "Sadly, due to the nature of this issue, I am unable to disclose that information despite the help you have rendered me."

Enyo shrugged. "It's fine. We were just happy to help."

"You are a very compassionate soul. Your silence on this matter is greatly appreciated." The woman bowed once more. "Now, if you'll excuse me, I must be off."

As the woman disappeared into the night, Enyo looked at Fellis.

"That was really strange," she said.

"Indeed." Fellis agreed. "Now, let's find a place to stay for the night. It is getting late and I, for one, would like to sleep."

"Agreed."

***

The next morning, Enyo decided to scout out the palace. That was why she woke up early, just as the dawn was breaking and most people were still asleep. She didn't want anyone getting in her way.

After reapplying her hair dye and using a spell to change her eye color, Enyo left the inn that she and Fellis were staying at and traveled through the paved roads.

Because it was still early in the morning, there weren't that many people up and about. Most of the people who were awake were the ones whose job was to set up their business—stall owners and vendors, clothiers and shopkeepers. They were the only ones getting ready to start the day.

As she walked passed a bakery, the scent of fresh bread wafted into her nose. Her stomach growled. She briefly thought about going in to buy some bread, but they didn't have much money. Unless there was a quest board somewhere that would allow her to earn cash, she would need to use their money sparingly.

Enyo hadn't thought of it before, but Alyssium was created much like a three-tiered cake. The first layer was the market and poor people's district, the second was the nobles' residence, and the third was Avant Heim. As she ascended a set of stairs that would take her up to the second level, this belief became solidified.

The nobles' residential district was a lot different from the market district. The houses down below were all basic square buildings made from brick and tiles. These buildings were far more opulent. They were graceful creations with sloping roofs and expansive gardens. Most of the houses had their own fountains and were lined with columns and statues. One house even looked like a palace that had been transplanted from another country entirely.

There weren't that many people outside in the noble district, either, which didn't surprise her as she imagined the nobles were quite lazy. Still, there were a few people out for an early morning stroll. She saw a noble woman decked out in a ridiculously gaudy dress walking her poodle. There were a pair of older nobles playing a game of chess in a park that she passed. However, aside from those few who seemed to enjoy the mornings, there was no one.

Or so she thought at first.

A crowd seemed to have gathered at one of the houses. This one was even more extravagant than most. It was a three-story home with a balcony and a porch. Four spires jutted from each quadrant as if they were points on a compass. Many windows dotted the exterior, though no one could see through them thanks to the curtains. A gate surrounded the mansion, and standing near the entrance were several dozen nobles.

Curious, Enyo drew close. She wanted to know what was going on here. The people were whispering, speaking in hushed tones. Enyo could barely make out their conversation.

"Did you hear…"

"… Dead…"

"Heard it was a murder."

Feeling more curious now, Enyo wandered up to the group. "Excuse me? But what happened here?"

The group turned as one. Enyo almost twitched when she noticed their disgusted faces as they gazed at her clothes, as if they were judging her based on what she wore.

"Is that a peasant?" one of them asked.

"What's a peasant doing here in the noble district?"

"Shoo! Shoo!"

Enyo didn't know how to take their reaction to her—if she should be upset, confused, or laugh because, technically, her position as the Dark Lady of the Dark Clan meant she had a higher status than them.

"Ah, it's you!" a familiar voice said.

Turning around, Enyo was greeted by the noble who'd tried to impress himself upon her last night. He was wearing a different set of clothes. That morning, his doublet was light blue and had shoulder pads that made his shoulders seem broader than they really were. His pants, which were the same color blue, were tight around his thighs, then puffed out near his calves before they were tucked into a pair of sturdy leather boots.

"Oh! You are, um… what was your name?" Enyo asked.

The man looked like he'd been shot in the chest with an arrow. "How could you forget my name?"

"Because you never gave me your name," Enyo said bluntly.

The noble blushed. "Is that so? You have my apologies, fair lady. My name is Alexander Tristane. It's a pleasure to make your acquaintance."

"Enyo," she introduced herself. "Do you know what happened here?"

"It appears someone has died," Alexander said. Leaning down, he cupped a hand to his mouth and whispered. "This mansion belongs to Patience—a member of the White Council. The White Council spends most of their time within Avant Heim, but they all have houses down here where they go to be alone. I heard he arrived late last night and was found dead by one of the servants early this morning."

After hearing this, anyone would have suspected foul play. The White Council were the leading magicians of Terrasole. From what little Enyo knew, their power was on par with the Dark Council, supposedly. Enyo didn't know if she believed that, but the White Council was the reason the Dark Council hadn't tried to subjugate humanity on their own.

"Do you suspect foul play?" she asked.

"That is the only thing I can think of that would cause Patience to die," Alexander said. "He was quite healthy and showed no signs of illness, yet he suddenly drops dead one night? If that isn't suspicious, then I don't know what is."

Enyo stayed for only a little bit longer, trying to glean what information she could from Alexander. Sadly, he knew very little, mere rumors and hearsay. When it was clear that she wouldn't be able to get any more knowledge from him, Enyo left and returned to the inn. She hadn't been able to study Avant Heim, but she'd learned something useful all the same. Fellis would want to know, too.

Her former maid was already awake when she returned. Enyo wouldn't have been surprised to learn that the woman had been awake when she'd left and merely stayed in bed because she didn't want to get up.

Fellis was sitting at a table located near the back of the inn's small tavern, a secure space where she could watch everyone who entered and exited the bar. She waved down Enyo when she saw her enter. As Enyo sat down, Fellis pushed a plate of fruits and toast in her direction.

"Thank you," Enyo said.

Fellis nodded as she drank from a cup of what smelled like really bold caffa. "Did you learn anything useful on your little outing?"

"Not really," Enyo admitted. "I was originally going to scope out Avant Heim, but then I found out that someone had been murdered last night and wasn't able to. I thought it would seem too suspicious if I started wandering around the palace grounds, so I left."

"Good idea," Fellis agreed. "What is our next plan of action going to be?"

"I want to learn more about that death," Enyo said. "While they might be unrelated, I think the death of a member of the White Council has something to do with our presence, or maybe Jacob's. We should investigate this further to find out what's going on."

"I will follow your lead, of course," Fellis said. "But first, let us have breakfast."

After breakfast, Enyo and Fellis traveled down the street, toward the town square where they had first learned that Jacob had been arrested. The town crier was there once again. He was not talking about Jacob this time.

"It has been confirmed that sometime last night, the great magician and member of the White Council, Patience, was murdered in his home." Murmurs broke out among the crowd. The town crier had to speak over their muttering, which grew louder with time. "Because of what happened, a new curfew has been put in place. No one is allowed to be outside once the sun has set. Anyone caught will be arrested."

The group dispersed after the crier finished speaking, though they continued to talk. There was an underlying current of fear. Enyo could see it in their eyes, in their faces, in the way they walked and talked. The White Council, unlike the Dark Council, was a well-known group. They were cornerstones of society. For one of them to die from something other than old age or disease was nearly unheard of.

"Security is going to be tight from now on," Fellis said.

Enyo didn't disagree. "That's going to make it difficult for us to move around."

"What do you propose we do?"

At Fellis's question, Enyo frowned and crossed her arms in thought. There wasn't much they could do. They couldn't afford to draw attention to themselves, which meant they only had one option right now.

"We need to blend in and wait until all the excitement has died down," she said at last.

"There's no telling how long that's going to take," Fellis pointed out.

"Then do you propose we catch the murderer?" asked Enyo. "That would not only put us in danger, but we might end up being exposed."

They walked down another street. This one held several shops, mostly clothiers and blacksmiths. Enyo could see black smoke rising from some of the chimneys. As she peered into one of the shops, an idea sprang to Enyo's mind.

"Let's change our attire to blend in better," she suggested.

Fellis raised an eyebrow. "Do we even have enough money for clothes?"

They did not. While she and Fellis had gone on several quests during their journey, most of that money had been spent on lodging and food. What little they had left was what she had saved up.

"Let's find the nearest bar," Enyo said. "I think I remember seeing a quest board at one of them. Let's see if we can take a quest or two to earn more money."

There was indeed a quest board located in front of the bars, one for each bar. Sadly, the quests offered were not those that paid well. They were not quests to slay monsters, protect caravans from bandits, or anything of the sort. These quests were simple. Ranging from courier quests to "find my lost pet" quests, they only paid, at most, fifty copper coins, enough for a single meal and nothing else.

Enyo and Fellis had split up to take on quests separately. Since they were so easy to complete, they could earn more by taking several quests at once and completing them on their own.

Most of the quests that Enyo had taken were quests to find missing pets, though there were a few that involved acting as a courier and one that even had her tending to a garden. In total, she completed sixteen quests for a total of eight silver coins.

Currency was relatively simple to work with. One hundred copper coins equaled one silver coin, and one hundred silver coins equaled one gold coin. A single silver coin was enough to stay at an inn for a single night.

Fellis had completed fifty-five quests and earned twenty-eight silver coins. Apparently, she had subtly used her magic to make other people work on her quests for her.

Since they had more than enough money thanks to Fellis, they traveled to a clothing store. By then, it was late in the evening. Curfew would be coming, so she and Fellis shopped quickly, buying clothing that was simple yet elegant.

Enyo, now wearing a simple black dress with a V-shaped cutout in the back and a slit on either side of her hips, sat at the bar, quietly nursing an ale that she only took an occasional sip of. Several feet away, Fellis was surrounded by several men who were cheering as she downed another mug of ale. She was, once again, having a drinking contest. Two men had already passed out, unable to keep up with the woman.

"Who's next?" she called with a grin. Several cheers sprang up as one cocky soul sat in the chair across from her. Fellis grinned as she held a full mug of ale in her hands and clicked it against the man's. "Bottoms up!"

Enyo sighed.

"Excuse me," a voice said as a familiar figure stepped in front of her. It was the paladin from before. "I couldn't help but notice that you look very familiar. Have we met before?"

Enyo played it cool. "I'm afraid I've never seen you before. Are you sure you're not talking about someone else?"

"Hmm."

The paladin leaned in closer. Enyo leaned back, but she tried to keep her expression nonchalant. After another moment, he stood back up and scratched at his head.

"I guess you're right. Your eye and hair color is different than the person I am thinking of. My apologies."

"It's fine." Enyo waved his apology off. "Who is this woman who looks like me? An old girlfriend?"

The paladin blushed at the mention of girlfriends. "I'm afraid not. The person I am looking for is a thief."

Enyo shifted. The gate key, which she'd attached to a chain around her neck, rested comfortably within the valley of her bosoms, hidden by her dress. "A thief, you say?"

"Yes, a vile thief who stole something important from Queen Alice." The paladin clenched his left hand and brought it up to his face. "That wretched woman... I can't believe anyone would be so horrible as to steal from her majesty. It's beyond reprehensible."

"Is that so?" Enyo asked, her right eyebrow twitching.

"Just so." The paladin nodded. "Sadly, I've not been able to continue my search."

"Why is that?"

"Because I had to bring Jacob Stone to Alyssium," he said seriously.

Enyo felt like someone had struck her with lightning magic. Her entire body jolted at the name. So this man really was the one who'd taken Jacob to Avant Heim, the reason that Jacob was in jail. She wanted to punch this man so hard. She held back, however, because she knew that they couldn't afford to cause trouble.

"Jacob... you are speaking of the hero, right? The one who was accused of betraying the crown and sentenced to life imprisonment?"

"He might have betrayed the crown, but at one point, Jacob was one of the greatest heroes our people have ever known," the paladin said seriously. "He used to go around rescuing all of the people who needed help, he journeyed through our land, righting wrongs and fighting for justice. He even defeated the Dark Lord, Alucard."

Enyo narrowed her eyes as a strange sense of competitiveness welled up inside of her. "Speaking of Jacob's journeys, did you hear about the time when he rescued a young woman who was dying from a fatal disease? He traveled deep into the Valley of the Dead, by himself, and brought back a rare flower that could cure it."

"What about the time when Jacob had to rescue an entire city by traveling deep into a volcano to fight a monster made entirely of lava?"

"That's nothing compared to when he journeyed through the Forest of Dreams for the sake of rescuing a single child."

"Saving an entire city is far more incredible than saving a single life."

"Saving one person shows that Jacob is willing to risk everything he has even for a single life. It shows his strength of character better than saving entire towns does."

As she argued with the paladin, Enyo became more and more sure of it. This man was a love rival. His obsession for Jacob was strong, so he must have been a rival for Jacob's affection. She'd heard about these, but she'd never expected to actually meet one— and to think that he was a guy to boot!

Their argument would have probably continued, and for hours at that, but the doors suddenly burst open and several knights walked in.

"Caslain!" one of them called out.

"What is it?" the paladin that she'd been arguing with asked. So his name was Caslain? She narrowed her eyes and engraved this name into her heart. She wouldn't let this man defeat her!

"We need you to come with us," the knight's voice was grave. "There's been another murder."

***

Enyo found out the next day that the person who was killed was another member of the White Council, and it was actually a double murder this time. The two people who were killed, Humility and Liberality, had been found dead in Humility's mansion. The town crier didn't say how they'd died.

Enyo suspected they'd been poisoned.

It was two days after the deaths of Humility and Liberality. The atmosphere of the city had changed completely. Where once there had been joy, now there was fear. People didn't stay in the streets for long. Vendors closed shops early. It seemed as if no one wanted to be outside anymore, and this was in spite of how all the council members had been killed in their own homes.

While it was in poor taste, Enyo and Fellis had taken advantage of the fear to increase their revenue. The increase in fear meant there were more quests that asked for bodyguard details. While the knights did their best, they could not be everywhere, and Queen Alice had declared that she also had to protect the common people. This hadn't endeared her to the nobles, but Enyo was thankful.

She and Fellis had made over fifty-five gold coins each for two days of protection detail. That was more than enough to last them for a few months. The person who had hired them was Alexander, the young noble who'd tried to woo Enyo. He still tried occasionally. However, Enyo shot him down every time. She did have to admire his persistence, though. It took a special kind of insanity to keep attempting the same thing over and over again and expect different results each time.

Three days after Humility and Liberality were killed, Enyo and Fellis were still acting as round the clock guards for Alexander.

The moon hung in the night sky. Enyo and Fellis had their own room to sleep in at Alexander's mansion, which was a lot nicer than the inn they had been sleeping at previously. Their room was right next to their employer's. That way they could arrive quickly if someone attacked him, though Enyo didn't think that would happen. The attacker had been killing members of the White Council, not nobles.

Sitting on her soft bed, Enyo looked out the window, admiring the stars and moon as she contemplated her situation. Even though she was glad to have found a way to earn money, it didn't bring her closer to her goal. She couldn't rescue Jacob like this.

Security around the palace has increased. We wouldn't be able to get within fifteen feet of the gates without getting arrested.

Jacob was somewhere inside of Avant Heim, locked away in a jail cell for treason. It was her fault that he was in there.

How am I supposed to rescue him?

Thinking on it, Jacob could probably have rescued himself, but he wasn't for some reason. Was he waiting for her? Or could it be that the queen had countermeasures put in place against Jacob's incredible strength? She wished she knew.

Lying on her own bed, which sat on the opposite side as Enyo's, Fellis, who lay on her stomach and had been flipping through the pages of a book, suddenly sat up.

"Something wrong?" Enyo asked.

"I detected a strong magic just now," Fellis said, marking the place in her book and standing up. "Come. Whoever is emitting that magic must be in trouble."

"I'm way ahead of you, Fellis."

Enyo threw on her clothing, dark black pants that fit her like a glove and were really comfortable, and a bodice that went over a black shirt. She also had a new set of vambraces, and the sheaths to her daggers were now around her thighs instead of her back. As she finished lacing up her boots, Fellis was already dressed and leaping out the window.

"H-hey! Wait for me!" Enyo shouted.

Clicking her tongue, she followed after Fellis, leaping out the window and landing on the ground in a crouch. Fellis was already several meters away. She put on a burst of speed, catching up to her companion. Together, they ran down the street, following where Fellis's senses took them.

"The magic is disappearing," Fellis announced as they rounded a corner.

"Then let's hurry," Enyo said.

Their race through the noble district took them to an empty park —almost empty, Enyo corrected when she noticed the figure lying on the ground and the creatures surrounding it. Wraiths.

Enyo didn't hesitate.

"Lux. Lumin. Luminous. Accendo!"

Light burst from Enyo's body as she felt a tug on her navel. It was like a brilliant star exploding. Illumination emitted from her body in a bright pulse that washed over the wraiths, who screeched in horror as they tried to run. Unfortunately for them, they were already trapped within her magic's sphere of influence. Their bodies turned to dust seconds before her attack ended.

Enyo knelt beside the inert figure. It was a woman with bronze skin. There were numerous lacerations covering her body, which emitted a dark purple miasma. It seemed her body had been contaminated with dark magic.

Chanting a healing spell under her breath, Enyo barely paid attention to Fellis as she placed her hands over the woman.

"How does she look?" Fellis asked.

"She's been poisoned," Enyo said. "There are two poisons running through her system. One is from dark magic, from the wraiths attack I'm guessing, but it seems there's another poison running through her bloodstream. It's going to take some effort to rid of them both."

Enyo frowned as she felt the constant drain on her magic. She'd cleared the miasma from the woman's body, but the poison was taking a lot longer. It must have been strong, or maybe it had simply been circulated through her body so much that it took time to extract it. Enyo sat on the ground, slowly healing the woman, until, with an exhausted sigh, she sat back.

"I'm done. Help me carry her to Alexander's."

"Okay."

Fellis scooped the woman up. Standing, she adjusted the female, who swayed limply in her arms. The bronze-skinned woman's head tilted back, forcing Fellis to readjust her again so it rested on her shoulder.

They journeyed back to Alexander's mansion, entering through the front door instead of a window. Enyo locked the door behind them. Then they traveled up to the bedroom that they shared and set the woman on the bed.

With the lighting from the fairy lamps providing a gentle illumination, Enyo was able to study the woman better. She was an exotic-looking woman. Her skin was dark bronze, and her lithe figure reminded Enyo of the dancers she sometimes saw at bars. Her clothing, a semi-translucent gown thrown over a pair of puffy pants and a strange cloth around her bust, also didn't strike her as something a noble would wear.

"I wonder who this woman is," Enyo said, frowning.

Fellis shrugged. "Your guess is as good as mine."

Since it was late, Fellis and Enyo went to bed. The woman was in Enyo's bed, so she and Fellis shared the other one. Sleep came easily. Enyo was exhausted.

When morning came, Enyo woke up to find that Fellis wasn't with her. The woman who she'd rescued was also gone. Standing up, she frowned upon realizing that she'd been sleeping in her clothes, which were now horribly wrinkled. As she stepped outside and wandered down the hall, she tried to smooth them out with little success.

Fellis was in the kitchen. The woman they'd rescued was with her. Both of them appeared to have been talking about something, but they stopped upon noticing her enter.

"Enyo," Fellis greeted. "It's a good thing you're awake. Kindness and I were talking about what happened last night. You should join us."

"Kindness?" Enyo questioned.

"Her name—well, her title," Fellis corrected.

"Uh huh."

"Kindness is the title that I go by," Kindness said. "I am a member of the White Council. Last night, someone managed to poison our water. All of my soldiers are dead. I only survived because I realized what was happening and used my magic to help counteract the effects, but then the wraiths attacked me. Speaking of which, I would like to extend my gratitude to you and Fellis for saving me. Had you not, I would have surely perished."

"You're welcome," Enyo said as she sat down. "Do you know who might have done this?"

"I have a hunch. However, I cannot talk about that here." Gesturing to Fellis, she continued. "Fellis has told me that you two are being employed here as bodyguards. I would like to hire you myself, should you be willing."

Enyo shrugged. "I don't mind, though you'll want to at least speak to our employer."

"That is fine," Kindness said. "When he wakes up, I shall demand that he relinquish your contract. Then we'll be off to Avant Heim."

It took everything Enyo had not to show her surprise. "We're going to the castle?"

"Yes, I have a matter of grave importance that I wish to discuss with Queen Alice," Kindness told her.

Enyo tried to contain her excitement. She would be going to Avant Heim, the place where Jacob was being held prisoner. Finally. Finally, she would be able to save him.

Hold on, Jacob. I'm coming.

That day, the world appeared just a little brighter.

***

Alexander had been quite flabbergasted when he'd come down that morning to discover Kindness sitting in his kitchen. After freaking out, which involved a lot of bowing, he'd told the woman that she could hire Enyo and Fellis. The woman had not hesitated and quickly employed the two as her bodyguards.

Which was how the two found themselves sitting in a carriage that would take them to Avant Heim.

Enyo was still somewhat dumbfounded—everything had happened so fast!—but she was also excited. She had been worried about how they were going to get into Avant Heim. It was truly good fortune that they had saved Kindness when they did.

They had already passed the front gate and were now being driven through a large garden. An array of flowers, green grass, and several bodies of water dotted the landscape. Glancing forward, Enyo glimpsed the massive spires and flying buttresses of Avant Heim.

"We'll be coming up on Avant Heim shortly," Alexander's butler said as he drove the carriage.

While everyone else seemed relatively calm, Alexander was shaking. Enyo didn't know if it was from nerves or something else, but she really thought he should calm down, lest he die of overexcitement.

The guards at the gate had let them in without a fuss once they'd learned who was inside of the carriage. She and Fellis had been given some looks, but no one had questioned them.

Stopping inside of a massive courtyard, the butler hurried to open the door. As Enyo stepped out, she looked at Avant Heim. She couldn't tell how many stories it was, but it must have been several dozen at least. A massive spire rose in the middle, ascending to form a point that seemed ready to pierce the heavens.

"Come along, you two," Kindness said, gesturing for her and Fellis to follow.

They strolled past several columns, which appeared to have no purpose other than decoration. When they reached the front door, a massive thing made of burnished wood, Kindness announced herself to the two guards stationed in front of it.

"I'm Kindness of the White Council. I'm here to see Queen Alice."

The guards saluted and opened the door for them. Kindness looked at her again, gestured, and then walked inside. She, Fellis, and even Alexander followed her into the castle.

"This is my first time here," Alexander confessed as they wandered the halls. "It's amazing, isn't it?"

"Yeah," Enyo agreed.

They walked along a marble hall. Beautiful columns supported an arched ceiling. To one side, glass windows made up almost all the wall, allowing an outside glimpse of the gardens. To the other was a beige wall decorated with artwork hanging from it and statues lining it at even intervals.

Enyo was surprised that no one had come to escort them, but as Kindness walked with a confident gait, she assumed that the reason was because they didn't need one.

"Kindness? Is that you?" an old man asked, walking out from around a corner. He wore the armor of a paladin, and despite his obvious age, he held himself with the confidence of an experienced warrior.

"Bayard," Kindness greeted. "I had not realized you were here. I thought you'd gone in search of the one who stole the otherworld gate key."

Enyo tried not to shift at the mention of the otherworld gate key, which still rested against her chest.

"The trail has gone cold, I'm afraid," Bayard admitted. "Besides that, unusual things have been happening. Monster sightings have been on the rise, and we're not getting reports from any of the towns bordering the Tenebrae Mountains. I've come back to report this to Queen Alice."

"I see. Trouble abounds everywhere, it seems."

As they spoke, Bayard looked back at her and Fellis. Confusion glazed his eyes. "I haven't seen any of these people around the palace before. Are they friends of yours?"

"No, we just met," Kindness said. "However, these two young women saved my life last night."

"Is that so? I guess there really is trouble afoot. It is a good thing there are still some kind people in this world."

"Indeed, there is. Now, if you'll excuse us, we really must speak with Queen Alice."

"I understand. I'll speak with you later."

Bayard left and the group continued on their way, until they reached another set of double doors. On the other side was a greeting room of some kind. The spacious interior contained the same opulence as everything else, but it was a bit more bare. Several meters away, on the opposite side of the room, sat a desk, and behind that desk was a beautiful woman with blonde hair and blue eyes.

The woman, who could only be Queen Alice, looked up as they approached her desk. Standing beside her was another woman, and her eyes widened when they landed on Enyo and Fellis.

"Kindness," Queen Alice said. "I am surprised you've come to speak with me like this. You've never done so before."

"Yes, I try not to bother you since I know how hard you work. However, events beyond my power to deal with have transpired, leading me to come and inform you of them," Kindness said, bowing.

Queen Alice frowned. "Tell me of these events, please."

Enyo listened intently as Kindness explained what happened before she and Fellis had arrived. "It happened while I was eating dinner; one of my maids became ill. She started coughing up blood and then she died. Soon after, all of my knights began dying as well. It appeared that someone had poisoned the well we use for water. As I had ingested the poison during dinner, I would have died myself, but I managed to use my magic to slow the poison down. I was attempting to reach the castle when I was attacked by wraiths. I would have died last night had these two not saved me."

"I see. I believe I understand the situation much more clearly now, and you two—" she directed her gaze toward Enyo and Fellis "—you have my thanks for saving Kindness."

"You're welcome," Enyo said. "Fellis and I were happy to help."

Queen Alice sent them a smile before redirecting her attention to Kindness. "It seems a lot has been happening as of late. The poison that you ingested must have been what killed the other White

Council members. However, we have no proof to show how they died. Not even an autopsy revealed the secrets of their death to us."

As she listened to everyone speak, Enyo realized that there was a lot going on. Assassins killing off White Council members, wraiths attacking people, and the knowledge that monster sightings were becoming more frequent. Would she even be able to rescue Jacob with all this commotion happening?

"Do you have any idea who could have done this?" Queen Alice asked at last.

Kindness shook her head. "I do not."

For just a moment, Queen Alice appeared exhausted. Her shoulders drooped, her body seemed to sag, and Enyo thought she saw bags under the woman's eyes. She must have been under a lot of stress.

The moment soon left, and Queen Alice straightened, as if she'd gained new life. Her eyes contained a determination that even Enyo found herself admiring. "We might not know who caused this, but we at least know how, and if we know how, it means we can neutralize the methods they are using. With luck, making it so they cannot poison anyone else should force them to confront us directly. When that time comes, we'll be ready."

"As you say."

"Now then..." Alice turned back to her and Fellis. "I hate to ask this of you, but as Kindness has vouched for you both, I would like to ask for your assistance. We could really use the help."

Enyo needed a moment to think about her request. If she helped out Queen Alice, she'd be close to Jacob and the otherworld gate. It would certainly up their chances of success. On the other hand, she'd be in constant contact with people who were essentially her enemy. If they found out that she had the otherworld gate key on her, then she was all but dead. In truth, it would probably be safer for her if she didn't help them, but...

Maybe... if I can help them with this, they'll let me and Jacob use the otherworld gate...

It was a long shot, but regardless, she wanted to believe in them, believe in the people who Jacob had saved when he was younger.

"We'll help you," Enyo said. Fellis looked at her with a frown but didn't say anything.

Alice's relieved smile made her feel like she'd done the right thing. "Thank you. Since you'll be helping us, I would like you to stay here in Avant Heim. I'll have Listy take you to a room. Once you've had a chance to freshen up, we'll all meet again and come up with a strategy to deal with this."

At the mention of her name, Listy stepped forward. "If you two could come with me, please."

Enyo looked at Fellis, who looked back. As Listy began walking, they quickly followed her, leaving behind Kindness and a completely out-of-his-depth Alexander, whose expression reminded her of someone after they'd been kicked in the balls.

The door closed behind them, and Listy walked off at a brisk pace. Enyo and Fellis quickened their stride to keep up.

"I didn't expect to see you again," Enyo said to the woman, who nodded and smiled.

"So you recognize me? That's impressive, considering I was wearing a cloak when we met." Listy paused for only a moment. "I had not expected us to meet either. It's strange how circumstances have brought us together once more. I almost feel as if it is fate."

Enyo wouldn't have gone so far as to say it was fate, but she said nothing about that. "So, you work in Avant Heim?"

"I am Queen Alice's personal maid," Listy said. "It is my job to do whatever Queen Alice asks of me, and also to make sure she does not overwork herself."

"She sounds like an overachiever," Fellis said.

"Queen Alice always works hard for the good of her people, but she has a very bad habit of neglecting her own health," Listy said as they ascended a flight of stairs.

Enyo glanced at the crimson rug underneath her feet. It was so soft her feet sank as she stepped on it. Even though she was used to living a life of luxury in the mansion that had been her prison, she was astounded by the sheer lavishness of Avant Heim.

They entered into a large hallway. As they did, Listy continued speaking. "With the nobles and many of the White Council not approving of Alice as a monarch, she has had to work three times harder than a king would have."

"Why a king?" asked Enyo.

"Because a queen is generally considered unsuitable for the position of monarch," Listy admitted. "The White Council claims it's because the last queen Terrasole had nearly led them to ruin after someone from the Dark Clan managed to infiltrate the upper echelons of our society and killed several important nobles at the time. However, the truth is that they simply do not approve of a female ruler."

Enyo had not realized that humanity also had this issue. The Dark Clan was typically a patriarchal race. That was why every Dark Lord without exception was male.

"How does Ali—Queen Alice deal with it?" asked Enyo.

Listy's smile was quite vicious as she said, "By putting the people who talk down to her for being a woman in their place. She's become adept at derailing every fallacious argument or dirty comment about her gender since accepting the crown. Those who continue to display belligerence are sent far away, where they cannot hinder her. You won't find a better ruler."

The room they were lead to was far larger than any room either of them had been in. It had two massive beds and several pieces of expensive furniture.

"This will be your room for the duration of your stay here," Listy said. "I'd love to speak with you both some more, when we have some free time, but for now, please enjoy yourselves."

"We will. Thanks!" Enyo said cheerfully.

Listy gave them one last smile before leaving. As the door closed behind her, Enyo went over to the bed and flopped down. She nearly shrieked when the bed tried to swallow her whole. Lying on a cloud would have been harder than this!

Fellis whistled as she slowly walked into the room. "This place really is nice, isn't it?"

"Nice is an understatement," Enyo muttered as she flipped onto her stomach and buried her face into the mattress. "How rich must someone be to have something so soft in a room they probably rarely use?"

"Well, this is Avant Heim," Fellis mused.

"Must be nice being a queen," Enyo said.

"Sounds like a pain in the katoosh if you ask me."

"I'm not even sure what a katoosh is," Enyo admitted before her thoughts shifted from light hearted to serious. "Fellis, once night comes, I want you to find Jacob."

"What shall I do if I find him?" asked Fellis.

"For now? Nothing." Climbing off the bed, Enyo strolled over to the window, and set her hands against the sill as she looked out. "We're in enemy territory now. We can't afford to act suspiciously."

"Besides, you also want to help them with their problems, right?" Fellis said with a knowing smile.

Enyo didn't deny Fellis' accusation. It was true. She wanted to help.

Looking out the window, Enyo could see practically all of Alyssium. The setting sun cast brilliant rays of orange and red light on the city, giving the sprawling community the appearance of a city on fire. It was beautiful, but the sight also made Enyo feel uneasy.

Somehow, she couldn't help but feel like something bad was going to happen.

∗

After Enyo and Fellis had been given a chance to settle in, Listy had returned and guided them to a dining room. There, Queen Alice and Kindness were waiting. Dinner had been served after they arrived, and the group discussed what to do about the current situation.

Unfortunately, there really wasn't a whole lot that could be done. The problem was that they had no idea who was behind these murders, so even if they knew how the White Council was being killed off, there was no way to catch them. That said, Queen Alice had sent out her knights to grab the remaining White Council members and escort them to the palace.

"If nothing else, I'd like to protect the White Council members who remain," Queen Alice said when Enyo asked about her decision.

The rest of their dinner had consisted of Queen Alice asking questions about themselves, but sadly, Enyo hadn't the foggiest idea of what to say. Fellis understood. It wasn't like she could tell Queen Alice that she was the daughter of the former Dark Lord.

Fortunately, Fellis had been prepared to field such questions.

"Lady Enyo comes from a small province near the Tenebrae Mountains," Fellis had told them. "Our home was attacked and destroyed, and so we've been on the move ever since."

Queen Alice had been touched upon hearing their story. She promised that Enyo and Fellis could stay in Avant Heim for as long as they needed. It seemed as if the queen was something of a bleeding heart.

Later that night, when everyone else had gone to sleep, Fellis had done as requested and snuck out of the bedroom that she and her charge shared. Because the door was guarded, Fellis had to sneak out through the window.

They were on the sixth floor, in one of the towers. As Fellis lowered herself out of the windowsill, she tried not to look down, already knowing what she would find.

The tower wall was made of large bricks. Despite there being numerous crevices, that did not mean she could climb down so easily. Locating places where she could find purchase was hard work. Her muscles strained as she slowly, cautiously, worked her way down the tower.

There were no guards at the bottom, which Fellis was thankful for, though that didn't mean she could let her guard down. While there might not have been any waiting at the tower's base, there were several patrolling the gardens and inside of the castle. Fellis used extra caution as she slipped past several guards. She was fortunate that the hedges were so large she could hide behind them.

Now, if I were a prisoner, where would I be?

Fellis didn't think the dungeon would be inside of the castle itself. It was probably located in a separate building. As she darted from hedge to hedge, always being sure to keep out of sight, Fellis eventually found what she believed might be the dungeon.

It was a tower, smaller than the one she and Enyo were residing in, though no less imposing. This one also looked a lot older. The bricks were faded and worn, moss grew around the bottom, and the whole thing seemed slightly dilapidated. Despite this, two guards were standing by the door.

What could be hiding in there, I wonder...

After centering herself, Fellis put on a seductive smile and strolled out from behind the hedge. The two guards started as they saw her. Fellis did not let them see her concern. She strolled forward with an exaggerated sway of her hips. Her smile widened when she noticed how both men were either staring at either her hips or her chest.

Men are so simple.

"Excuse me," Fellis said, putting on her best *I'm an innocent maiden* voice. "I'm Queen Alice's guest, but I seem to have gotten lost and can no longer find my room." Her eyes began to glow as she trapped the two men with Mind Manipulation. "Do you think you can help me by pretending I was never here? I'd be rather embarrassed if Queen Alice found out about this."

"Sure," the guard on the left said.

The other guard nodded. "We'll do anything you ask of us."

"You're too kind," Fellis said. "In that case, would you mind if I asked whether or not this place is where Jacob Stone is currently being held?"

The left guard nodded. "It is. He's currently being held in the lowest level of the dungeon."

"Thank you," Fellis said. "Now, I would like it if you two could forget that this conversation ever took place—oh! And could you please let me inside?"

The right guard opened the door for her, and she walked past them and inside. Fellis took a moment to look around. She was in a staircase. One side went up and the other down. The guards had mentioned that Jacob was being held in the lowest levels.

Down it is.

With her footsteps sounding ominously loud as she walked down the stairs, she traveled in a downward spiral until reaching a small wooden door. She opened it a crack and peeked inside. There were two guards. They were sitting at a table, playing what appeared to be a game of cards.

This is going to be more difficult than the other two guards.

Mind Manipulation was tricky in that it could be broken if the people you were controlling suspected that something was wrong. Of course, she could overpower their minds, but that still required time to enact her magic. Being in a dungeon when she wasn't supposed to was definitely suspicious. There was a good chance that her mind magic wouldn't work, or wouldn't work effectively, especially since she needed to ensnare them both at the same time.

I can't afford to knock them unconscious either.

She might be able to slip past them. Neither of them were paying much attention to anything but their game. If she could somehow make them focus completely on each other, or maybe start fighting each other, then she—

"Who are you? What are you doing here?" a voice behind her asked.

Fellis spun around and, her heart hammering in her chest, she smiled at the armored knight before her. "Hello, I'm no one important. I'm just looking around."

It was interesting to see someone resist her mind control. Their fingers would twitch and their eyes would flutter as if fighting against a headache. This man was no different. However, since she was only focusing on him, and his will didn't seem terribly strong, he eventually succumbed.

"I understand. You're just looking around."

"That's right. Are you here to change the guard?"

"Yes…"

"I see. Do you have someone else coming soon to replace the other guard?"

"No…"

"In that case, maybe you can help me. Would you be a dear and help me subdue your partner once the knight you replace leaves?"

"Of course."

"Thank you."

As the knight she'd trapped in her mind control entered the dungeon, Fellis jumped up the wall. She placed her hands on one wall and her feet on the other, holding herself against the ceiling as she waited for one of the knights to leave. It was hard. Her arms and legs shook, and her abdominal muscles shivered as she flexed them.

The door beneath her opened. A knight walked out, his armor clinking. He didn't look up as he went up the stairs, disappearing as he rounded the curve.

Fellis dropped back down to the floor with a grimace. Her arms and legs felt stiff now. She did her best to stretch out the kinks before walking into the dungeon. The knight whom she'd ensnared saw her walk in. He stood up and, without warning, sent the other knight to the ground.

"What the f—what are you doing?!" the other knight screamed before he was captured in a strong grapple. He struggled to break free, but in that moment, Fellis grabbed his chin and forced him to look into her eyes.

"Would you please stop struggling?"

Despite asking politely, the knight still continued to struggle—at least for a little while. His struggling eventually subsided and then ceased altogether. She smiled when his eyes glazed over.

"Good. Now, you two go back to standing guard. Please just forget you ever saw me here."

"Okay," the one in back said.

"We can do that," the other said.

"Good."

As the two knights sat back down, Fellis wandered deeper into the dungeon. It honestly didn't look like much of a dungeon to her. Sure, it was dark and old and rusty, but it was thousands of times better than the dungeons in the darklands. She couldn't even feel a draft in here.

All the cells were empty. Fellis guessed they weren't used often. It made sense. Alucard had once told her that humans were soft-hearted. They could rarely bring themselves to imprison people. As she reached the end of the dungeon, she finally found Jacob. He was laying on a small cot, his feet hanging off the edge.

"You're looking comfortable," Fellis commented.

"I'm very comfortable," Jacob shot back, sitting up in bed and sending her a look. "What are you doing here? Where's Enyo?"

"Worried about your woman?"

"Yes. Is that wrong of me?"

Fellis needed a moment to contain her surprise. "No, there's nothing wrong with that. In either event, Enyo is fine. She is currently residing within Avant Heim, to help Queen Alice with her investigation."

It was amusing to watch the way Jacob's face scrunched up as if she'd just said something amazingly stupid. "Is that some kind of joke?"

"I assure you this is no joke," Fellis said before kicking off into an explanation of what had happened up to this point. The longer her explanation went on, the closer Jacob's jaw came to dropping. By the time she'd finished, his expression reminded her of a troll being strangled by its own loincloth.

"That's... a lot to take in," Jacob admitted. "I had no idea there was so much going on outside."

"Speaking of outside, may I ask why you haven't broken out of here yet?" Fellis inquired. "These bars are not strong enough to hold you, so why are you still in here?"

Jacob shrugged. "Where would I go? If I broke out now, not only would I be hunted, but the chances of me getting into Avant Heim again would be close to zero."

"I see. So you are remaining here to await an opportunity for you and Enyo to make your escape through the otherworld gate."

"That's pretty much it."

That was a smart move. She was impressed by his foresight. He wasn't just sitting around for no reason, accepting what must have been the harshest form of betrayal ever, but was instead waiting for the right moment to escape.

"Very well. I'll let Enyo know what is happening."

"Thank you."

With nothing left to do, Fellis left, exiting the dungeon the same way that she got in. None of the guards stopped her. The next day, they would not even remember that she'd been there.

CHAPTER 4 - LUSTFUL INTENTIONS

Enyo woke up early the next morning. Fellis was already awake, or perhaps she'd never fallen asleep. She found her former servant sitting on the windowsill, looking at the ground below, her expression furrowed as if in deep contemplation.

"Fellis... morning..." Enyo yawned.

"Good morning." Fellis sent a smile her way. "I was quite surprised to find you asleep when I returned from visiting Jacob last night. I would have expected you to be up and eagerly awaiting to hear news about your boyfriend."

"Could you please stuff it?" Enyo asked. "Just tell me how Jacob was."

Fellis chuckled. "He is doing well, from what I could see. Nothing seems to be wrong with him, and it's not like he couldn't escape whenever he wanted to. When the time comes to leave this world, he will join up with us."

Despite having already suspected that to have been the case, Enyo still felt as if a huge weight had been lifted from her shoulders. They were in the perfect position now. All of them were in Avant Heim, where the otherworld gate was located. There was only one thing left to do.

"While we help out the queen with her problem, we should use this opportunity to locate the otherworld gate. Once we know where it is, we'll have Jacob break out of the dungeon, activate the gate, and leave this world behind."

"That seems like a sound plan," Fellis agreed.

A knock sounded at the door. Enyo clammed up as a moment of panic struck her. Had the person on the other side heard them talking? Calming her racing heart, she took a deep breath and said, "Come in."

The door opened and Listy came in, offering them both a smile and a polite bow. "Queen Alice has asked that I bring you to her. Breakfast has been prepared, and she would like you to join her and Kindness."

"Thank you. We'll go there in just a moment. Would you mind if we took a second to wash up?"

"Not at all. I'll be waiting outside. Come out when you're ready."

Giving them a bow, Listy exited the room, the door closing behind her with a soft click. Enyo sighed in relief. It seemed the servant hadn't heard anything.

She and Fellis took a quick fifteen minutes to wash and get dressed. There was a basin of water they could use to clean themselves with. It wasn't anywhere near as pleasant as the baths, but this was placed within every room because sometimes a bath was just not feasible.

Enyo also had her hair dye reapplied and recast the spell on her eyes. It was a good thing Listy hadn't been looking at her from up close, or she might have noticed that her eyes had been pink instead of brown. Exiting the room, they found Listy standing outside just like she'd said.

"We're ready," Enyo said.

"In that case, please follow me."

As they walked off, Enyo immediately noticed that they weren't traveling to the same place as yesterday. The route they were taking was in the opposite direction.

"Has anything changed since yesterday?" asked Enyo.

"If you are speaking of the things that Queen Alice discussed with you, then there have been a few changes." Listy paused as if gathering her thoughts. "The other members of the White Council all arrived last night and were informed of what happened. Since they're the ones in danger, it has been decided that they will be living in the west wing until the killer has been caught. They have rooms there in either event, and it won't deter their work."

"How did they take that?" asked Fellis.

"Justice and Abstinence took it well. Chastity did not. He complained quite loudly. I'm honestly surprised you were not awakened by his shouting."

"I'm a heavy sleeper," Enyo joked.

Listy smiled. "Indeed."

They arrived on a balcony overlooking another garden. There was a circular table set up next to a magnificent balustrade made of gleaming marble. Queen Alice and Kindness were already sitting down. The other two empty chairs must have been for her and Fellis.

"Good morning, you two," Queen Alice greeted. "Please, come and sit down. I trust you both slept well?"

"We did, thanks," Enyo said as she and Fellis sat down. Listy walked to the table, grabbed an ornate teapot, poured tea into two silver cups, and then presented it to her and Fellis. Then she stood beside Queen Alice, hands clasped in front of her.

There was a smorgasbord of food arrayed on a three-tiered tray in the center of the table. Danishes filled with cream cheese and fruit fillings, muffins, and various treats sat sparkling on the tray. Enyo's mouth practically watered at the sight, but she held back and carefully grabbed only two Danishes instead of the whole platter.

"How are you feeling, Kindness?" Enyo asked before taking a bite of her muffin. Blueberry. Delicious.

"I am doing well," Kindness said. "All of my wounds have healed and I was able to sleep peacefully, though I could have done without Chastity's whining."

"I heard that the other White Council members showed up last night," Fellis said. Unlike Enyo, who tried to eat with grace, she had no issue shoveling food into her mouth.

"You heard correct," Queen Alice said. "They will be joining us for our meeting today. Since this situation involves them, we can't afford to exclude them."

They spoke for a little while longer—small talk about subjects of little importance. Enyo had never done small talk before, but it was interesting to talk about things that didn't involve life or death situations. She also learned a bit more about the two: Queen Alice and Kindness.

Kindness was actually from another country, one that could only be reached by crossing the sea. She'd come to Terrasole seeking to escape a war that had ravaged her lands. The clothing she wore was in honor of her homeland.

On the other hand, Queen Alice liked to complain and make wisecracks about the nobility, especially the men. She told them stories about all the men who tried to claim her heart and were subsequently brow beaten until they realized she had no intention of getting married. It was fun.

"I'll eventually have to produce an heir," Alice said. "However, when I do, it will be at my convenience and with someone who I think is worthy of siring a child with me. Thus far, only one person has shown themselves worthy of that honor."

She said nothing of the man who'd "proven himself worthy." Enyo wondered if she was talking about Jacob, but she didn't ask. It would have been rude to pry. Also, there was a small part of her that feared the answer.

After breakfast, Queen Alice and Kindness went off to discuss political matters. Since Enyo wasn't involved in those, she and Fellis were left to their own devices.

Having grown used to being in near constant danger, or at least having something to do, Enyo found that she was very bored. She wanted to do something. She wanted to save people, face danger, and go on adventures. All this waiting around was annoying.

In an effort to quell her boredom, Enyo wandered the castle. Avant Heim was a big place—emphasis on the big. There were so many rooms that she couldn't help but wonder what Queen Alice did with them all.

As she was turning a corner, someone else appeared in front of her. Despite her shock, Enyo still responded with instincts bread from constant battle. She spun on the balls of her feet. She glided past the man who'd nearly ran her over. Behind her, Fellis stopped several paces away, avoiding the entire incident.

"I'm sorry," Enyo apologized. "I didn't see you."

The man, a young man with dark hair and black eyes, held up a hand. "There is no need," he said, his hair swaying as he shook his head. "I should have been paying more attention to where I was going. I hadn't expected anyone else to be wandering around like I was."

"Okay. Well, in that case, I'll bid you a good day," Enyo said, prepared to leave.

"H-hold on a moment!" the man practically shouted. She looked back at him. He licked his lips. "Perhaps you would like to accompany me? I've stayed in Avant Heim enough times that I know my way around fairly well, but you look new. I could show you around."

Enyo debated the idea of telling this man off. Truth be told, she didn't like the way he was looking at her. She felt naked. On the other hand, she couldn't dismiss someone merely because they made her feel uncomfortable. Besides that, if he did try something, she could always stab him with her daggers.

"I don't mind," Enyo finally said. "Fellis?"

Fellis shrugged. "Whatever you want. I'm just tagging along."

"Great!" the man clapped his hands together. "In that case, I'll show you around."

The man, who Enyo soon learned was Chastity—the White Council member who Queen Alice had complained about—took her on a basic tour of the castle. While showing her the various rooms and wings, he tried to link their arms together. She jerked her arm out of his grip. He frowned, but when she raised a challenging eyebrow, his agitated expression was replaced with a smile.

Avant Heim had a grand total of six wings: north, south, east, west, and then the towers, which were considered their own wings. Most of the wings consisted of lounges and bedrooms. Those were used to entertain guests. According to Chastity, a lot of nobles visited the castle from all over Terrasole and would stay in these wings with their family and servants.

"I haven't seen you in Avant Heim before," Chastity tried to make conversation. "I'm assuming you are not a new servant, but someone who has business with Queen Alice?"

Enyo nodded. "That's right. Fellis and I saved Kindness when someone tried to assassinate her."

Chastity twitched. Was he concerned about Kindness, or perhaps the knowledge that Kindness had been attacked made him fear that he would be next? Enyo didn't know.

"Yes, I had heard about the attack, though I had not heard that you rescued her. Thank you for saving her. Kindness is a valued compatriot."

"You're welcome."

It took some time, but Enyo finally managed to separate herself from Chastity, who kept trying to touch her. A brush to the back of her hand with his knuckles, a hand on the small of her back. He might have thought he was being subtle. However, subtlety clearly wasn't his strong point.

After escaping from his presence with a flimsy excuse, she and Fellis ran into Listy. The maid greeted them with a polite bow and said, "I have been looking for you two. The meeting is about to start soon, and Queen Alice wanted you to be there."

"Lead the way," Fellis said with a wave of her hand.

The meeting room was in the west wing; Enyo remembered from when Chastity had given her the tour. Everyone was already there. Queen Alice sat at the head of a long table. Kindness sat on her left, while an old man with so many wrinkles his face seemed to sag sat on her right. Chastity was also there, and he waved when he saw her. She waved back to be polite.

There was one other person sitting at the table. Like the one next to Queen Alice, he was aging and looked frail. His twig-thin arms made her think they'd snap at the slightest movement. Despite this, he grabbed his long beard with his frail hands and stroked it while contemplatively eying her with narrowed blue eyes.

Bayard was also present. He, along with a surprised Caslain, stood behind Queen Alice.

"Good, you two are here," Queen Alice said. "Now we can start the meeting. As you all know, three members of the White Council have been killed. Kindness would have joined them were it not for Enyo and Fellis's aid. Once again, you have my eternal gratitude."

"You're welcome," Enyo said as she and Fellis sat together. They were as far from Chastity as they could be without making it obvious.

Alice nodded back to her before she continued. "Thanks to Kindness, we have learned that Liberality, Humility, and Patience were killed by a poison. I've sent one of my alchemists to check the water from the well at Kindness's manor. We should be getting the results within a day or two."

"So, you're saying that someone has poisoned our wells?" the old man close to Queen Alice asked.

"That is what we believe, Abstinence."

"That's preposterous." Abstinence scoffed. "All of our manors are protected by a personal barrier. The only way someone could get past it without us knowing was if they had an intricate understanding of the barrier. No one has such knowledge except for other members of the White Council."

"You don't know that," Kindness rebutted in a calm voice. "The fact that three of us were killed and I was almost killed is proof enough that someone can get past our barriers."

"Bah! You four were probably just foolish enough to allow someone into your manor without knowing they were trying to kill you. I'm not so simple-minded as to allow an enemy into my house."

Kindness narrowed her eyes. "To not only insult the dead but also insult me to my face. You, Abstinence, are an idiot."

"What was that?!"

"For your information, I did not allow anyone into my home," Kindness continued. "I had been home alone with my servants and knights. There was no one else. Yet I still fell prey to poison."

"Perhaps it was one of your servants."

Kindness narrowed her eyes. "Are you accusing me of having poor choice in servants?"

"I didn't want to say it out loud, but..."

"An ignorant fool such as yourself has no right to say anything about me," Kindness snapped. "All of my servants have been serving me faithfully for over ten years now. What's more, all of them died because they were also poisoned. I'll not have you speak poorly of the deceased anymore!"

Before the argument could progress further, the other old man —who Enyo guessed was Justice—spoke up. "Both of you should cease arguing at once. I know that tempers are running high due to what happened, but that's no excuse to lose your composure."

"My… apologies," Abstinence muttered.

"I apologize as well," Kindness said.

Justice nodded. "What we are dealing with right now is an unprecedented crisis. Since the founding of the White Council, no one has ever managed to kill so many of us with such trickery. And while I do not wish to take sides, Abstinence does bring up a good point. The barriers around our manors are impenetrable save for three ways. One: they use an overwhelming amount of force. Two: they slip through the barrier, which can only happen if someone has intimate knowledge of how these barriers work. And three: they received permission to enter from the homeowner."

Enyo knew a little about barriers. There had been a barrier around her mansion when she was younger. She'd never studied it in depth, but she knew that it was designed to render the mansion invisible to anyone who was not tuned into the runes. According to Fellis, her father had set it up as a way of keeping the Dark Council from finding her.

"Option one is out of the question. We'd have known if someone destroyed a barrier that way. That leaves just option two and option three. The only people who understand how the barriers work are myself, Humility, and I believe you, Chastity, are also studying the inner workings of rune barriers."

"I am, but I'm still far behind the both of you." Chastity rubbed the back of his head. "They are a lot more complicated than I initially thought."

"Indeed they are." Justice nodded. "Now, since only three people even understand the barrier, we can rule out option two. That leaves only option three. Kindness…" Justice fixed her with a look.

"I know that you are not the type to just accept anyone into your home. Is there someone you can think of who might have been acting strange? Perhaps the person was under mind magic."

Kindness gained a thoughtful look. Enyo glanced at Fellis, who subtly shook her head, signifying that she did not know any other mind magic users. The only one who could have come close to that sort of magic was Darkness, but she was dead.

"I do not believe so," she said at last. "At least, not that I know of, but I will admit that I hadn't been paying much attention to everyone except my head maid."

"We feel at ease in our own home, so it is difficult sometimes to notice when something is amiss," Justice assured her. "That said, since you do not know if someone of your household was being manipulated, we are back to square one."

The group continued to speak, but Enyo stopped paying attention at that point. She wasn't interested in listening to them discuss the issue. All she wanted to hear was what they planned to do from now on. Beside her, Fellis was leaning her head on her hand, her eyes closed as she nodded off.

Enyo only started paying attention again when Queen Alice said, "Let's take a recess and return after we've had a chance to eat and freshen up."

She stood up with everyone else, tapping Fellis on the shoulder to wake her up, and then left with her yawning former servant in tow. The others also left one at a time. Kindness caught up to the pair as they were walking down the hall.

"You sure were quick to leave," Kindness said. "Were you two bored? You looked like you were about to fall asleep."

"I wasn't that interested in what anyone was saying since they didn't come up with a solution to our problem," Enyo admitted shamelessly.

"I was up late last night," Fellis said.

"Is that so?" Kindness shook her head. "Either way, I wanted to speak with you about—"

Before she could finish, a loud clapping noise like thunder struck them def. Enyo screamed as she placed her hands over her ears. She could feel warm liquid pouring from them. It felt like someone was blowing a horn in her ears!

It took nearly a minute for Enyo to realize the sound had stopped. Slowly, as if afraid it would start up again, she released her ears and opened her eyes. She was kneeling on the ground. Attempting to stand up, Enyo very nearly doubled over again as everything spun around. She pressed a hand to her face as if trying not to vomit.

"That sound..." Fellis groaned next to her. "W-what was that?"

Kindness slowly climbed to her feet, her knees shaking and blood pouring from her ears. "T-that was the sound of someone breaking through the defensive barrier around Avant Heim. Someone is attacking us!"

Hearing that, Enyo forced herself to stand up. Her knees wobbled, her legs shook, and she even had to clench her butt cheeks to remain standing. The urge to vomit was overwhelming, but she stood and unsheathed her daggers. Fellis had also risen to her feet and was pulling out her whip.

"Come on," Enyo said, ignoring the way her ears rung from the sound of her own voice. "We need to find Queen Alice and the others."

The last place they had seen Queen Alice was the White Council meeting chamber, so they started their and worked their way along the route they believed the queen had taken.

As they were moving down a hallway, something burst out from the other side. It scrambled toward them on four legs. Its crimson eyes glowed with malicious intent and its midnight fur bristled. It had two heads. Two rows of razor sharp teeth were revealed as the creature opened its mouth and howled. That seemed to have been a signal, for four other beasts followed.

"What are these things?!" Kindness finally lost her composure and screamed.

"Orthos!" Fellis shouted in shock. "These are beasts from the darklands!"

"What?!"

"They're coming!"

Enyo fought against a smile as she wreathed her blades in light magic. Her blood was pumping stronger than ever. She struggled to control her bloodlust. She couldn't allow it to make her reckless.

The orthos were on them, the one in front lunging at her while two others leapt over it. Enyo went down, bending backward until she was lying on her back. The orthos missed. She then stuck her blade out as it passed over her, grinning in satisfaction as the blade cut through the creature's stomach like a hot knife through water.

It tumbled to the ground. Then it skidded into two other orthos, which had been about to attack Kindness and Fellis. Enyo scrambled to her feet as the one that had remained behind lunged for her. She leapt over it, flipping as she landed on its back. Without wasting a moment, she stabbed her right blade into the creature's neck, severing its spine and causing it to collapse. The orthos whined as its body twitched several times before falling still.

"Orthos are weak against light magic!" Enyo shouted at the two. "You need to use light magic to slay them!"

"I don't know light magic!" Kindness shouted as she thrust out her hands. Several strange balls appeared and slammed into an orthos, pelting it like hailstones smacking against a window.

The orthos roared, seemingly angry, and then charged at Kindness, who gritted her teeth as she wove her hands through the air in a complicated fashion.

"Pentro. Perfringo. Percutio."

A spear formed in the air and struck the orthos in the eye. Blood spurted as the spear impaled it. Despite this, the creature continued rushing at Kindness, its own drooling mouths opening wide.

"Volnus. Vulnus. Stigma." Enyo chanted.

There was a pull on her navel as a crescent of light shot from one of her daggers and sliced into the orthos. The creature howled in pain and rage as it tumbled to the ground. Enyo leapt from the dead orthos and charged at the one that she'd hit, channeling magic through her left dagger, which she used to slice through one of the heads.

Enyo felt a moment of resistance. Then her dagger was going straight through it. Blood gushed from the open wound and splattered against the ground. The other mouth howled in pain, but Enyo silenced it by thrusting a dagger through its skull. She pulled her weapon out as the creature shuddered before dying.

"Enyo!" Fellis shouted. "I could... use a little help!"

Her friend was in trouble. She stood on top of the orthos. One of its mouths was sealed shut by her whip. However, she only had one whip, so the other head was snapping at her, though, more often than not, it chomped down on the other head's ear.

Springing into action, Enyo unleashed another crescent at the orthos, which sliced into its unbound head. The monster jerked violently. Fellis yelped as she was thrown off it, but she still managed to twist her body and land on its feet.

Wanting to finish the creature off while she had the chance, Enyo swung both blades at the same time. Two crescents shot at the orthos. One sheared through its head, which fell to the floor with a meaty thud. The other nearly missed. A gash appeared on the underside of its throat. Crimson ichor spilled onto the ground as the monster spasmed and twitched. Enyo rushed up, leapt into the air, and then stabbed both blades into its head, killing it.

"You... you're very talented with light magic," Kindness muttered, her breathing heavy. Sweat poured from her brow, which she tried to wipe away with little success.

"Thank you," Enyo said, regaining her breath. She hadn't expended much energy, but all of that jumping around was kind of tiring.

"We need to get moving," Fellis said. "We have to find the queen."

Enyo and Kindness agreed. Together, they went off in search of Queen Alice. Yet as they hurried to find Queen Alice, a bad premonition came over Enyo.

Call it a hunch, but she had a feeling that this situation would not end well.

***

They found Queen Alice battling against several orthos alongside Listy and the rest of the White Council. It was an impressive sight to behold.

The group was in the great hall. Queen Alice wielded a sword with an expertise that could match the best paladin's. She dodged attacks before they came, almost as if she could see into the future. Then she would attack the orthos with precise strikes that, on anything else, would have killed it by now. Unfortunately, orthos were invulnerable to everything except light magic and certain specialized magics. Physical attacks were meaningless.

"Listy!" Queen Alice shouted.

"I'm on it!" Listy leapt into the air, over the orthos, chanting something under her breath. Enyo couldn't hear her, but what happened next shocked her.

Listy thrust out her middle and index fingers. Nothing seemed to happen at first, but then, as if some invisible blade had impaled the orthos, a large hole appeared in its body. Blood burst from its back and spilled from its stomach. The beast roared in agony before, just like last time, Listy thrust out her fingers again, this time at its left head. Blood, bones, and brain matter flew out from the hole as the orthos slumped to the ground.

Standing side by side, Justice and Abstinence attacked two other orthos, which couldn't seem to get close to them. The reason was because of Abstinence, who appeared to be a defensive magic user. He'd chant something in a booming voice, and then a barrier made of the purest silver would spring into existence. The orthos would slam into it, bounce off as if launched into the air, and land on the ground hard enough to dent it. The area around them was already filled with pock marks. When the beasts hit the ground, Justice would launch his own attack.

"Atero. Perdo. Diruo. Concido. Erado!"

Justice pointed a wand at the orthos, which fell to the floor and began thrashing around. Enyo didn't get what was happening at first. Then she saw it. The orthos's skin was sloughing off its body. Large amounts of skin seemed to melt, becoming ooze as it dripped to the floor. It wasn't just skin, though. Its muscles, bones, organs, everything was being liquefied. Soon, the orthos was nothing but a puddle on the once sparkling marble floor.

A distance off, Bayard roared much like a beast as he shoulder-shoved an orthos. Much to Enyo's surprise, the monster went flying, slamming into a large column, which shattered upon impact. For an old man, he was stupidly strong.

Bayard shifted into a low stance, with his blade in front of him, pointed at the beast as it climbed back to its feet and growled. He muttered under his breath. Then, elongating at speeds that made Enyo blink, his sword grew increasingly larger and stabbed into the orthos. Sadly, the only thing it seemed capable of doing was growing longer. The blade couldn't penetrate the monster's bristly hide, which acted as armor against physical and most magical attacks.

"Take this!" Caslain shouted as he descended from the sky.

Enyo would have wondered how he'd gotten so much height, but then he slammed into the orthos like a twelve-ton boulder. The creature couldn't even howl in pain. A loud snapping sound echoed across the room as the monster's bones broke like brittle twigs. The orthos released unusual gurgling noises as blood poured from its mouth, though the noises soon stopped coming as its body went limp.

Well... Enyo blinked. *That's one way to kill it.*

Even though the group had done well, there were still more orthos to deal with. What's more, it seemed as if Chastity was missing.

Enyo didn't bother looking around for the White Council member. She infused her daggers with light magic and jumped into the fray. Since Queen Alice and Listy were the people she cared about more, she raced toward them. They were fighting against two more orthos. Queen Alice was dodging their attacks like she could predict the future, while Listy use her magic to try and punch holes through the monsters. Sadly, it seemed the orthos had cottoned on to what they were doing. They dodged all Listy's attacks.

"Volnus. Vulnus. Stigma."

The tug on Enyo's navel preluded the white crescent of energy that shot out of her dagger and struck one of the orthos dead on. A pained howl resounded through the Great Hall, the crescent attack slicing into the orthos's left flank. Enyo didn't stop there. She chanted again, brought down her other dagger, and sent another crescent that hit the same spot. It sheared through the orthos's body, slicing it in half.

"Queen Alice!" Enyo rushed to the woman's side. "Are you all right?"

"Yes, I am fine," Queen Alice said. "I'm pleased to see that you, Fellis, and Kindness are uninjured as well."

As they spoke, Listy finally managed to finish off her foe. She waited until it had lunged at her, leapt onto its back, and used her magic to pierce both its necks. The attacks had gone straight through. The orthos died almost instantly.

"I've never seen creatures like these before," Queen Alice said as she toed one of the orthos.

"It's an orthos, your majesty," Justice said as he and Abstinence walked up to her. "They are creatures from the darklands. The Dark Clan often uses them as attack mounts. I am surprised to see them here. How did they get into Avant Heim? And why was the alarm in the city not sounded?"

"Do you think someone could have used summoning magic?" Queen Alice asked.

"It's not impossible," Justice admitted reluctantly. "But for someone to break through the barrier around Avant Heim and summon so many orthos, they would have to be unbelievably powerful. I do not think there is a single person in the entire world who has the power to do such a thing save the Dark Lord."

"Yet we can't deny that it happened," Queen Alice said. "By the way, where is Chastity?"

"The last I saw, he was running from several orthos," Abstinence said, scoffing. "He said something about drawing them away, but I think he was just being a coward."

Even as Abstinence spoke, several large explosions echoed throughout the Great Hall. Enyo couldn't pinpoint where they came from, as it sounded like they were coming from everywhere. The floor and walls and ceiling all shook. She and the others were almost knocked to the floor.

"W-what is that?" asked Enyo.

"That must be Chastity," Justice said. "His magic is called Havoc. It's the ability to create widespread destruction. I'm not sure how it works, but it's a powerful magic."

"I see," Bayard said as he sheathed his blade. Caslain was standing beside him. "That is indeed a powerful magic. I'm guessing he drew as many enemies to him as he could in order to take them out away from us. That way we wouldn't get caught in the crossfire."

"If that's how you want to see it, then go right ahead and think that way," Abstinence said. "I know the truth. Chastity might be a powerful magician, but he's also a coward. He's not the type of person to fight against monsters like this head-on."

As he spoke, the door opened and Chastity walked in, looking a little worse for wear. His clothing was ripped, he was bleeding from a head wound, and he walked with a limp. There was a strange gleam in his eyes.

"Chastity," Justice said, frowning. "I see that you've been injured in your battle. Is all well?"

"No, all is not well," Chastity said. "I just learned a shocking truth. I know who let these creatures in." He pointed at Enyo. "It was her."

"What?" Enyo was stunned. She had no idea how to respond to that, or indeed, where this man had even come to such a conclusion.

"Did you hit your head or something?" Fellis asked. "Where would you come up with such an asinine idea?"

"Is it really asinine, or are you merely saying that because you're her accomplice in all this?" asked Chastity.

"Those are some very heavy accusations," Queen Alice stated in a stern, unwavering voice. "I hope you have proof to back up your claim."

"I do," Chastity said. "Right now, that girl is carrying the otherworld gate key on her person. It's currently attached to a chain around her neck."

Enyo felt like she'd suddenly been put on the spot when everyone turned to stare at her. She tried to think about how she should respond to Chastity's accusation. Should she deny it? If she did, then it might come back to bite her. Plus, everyone would now be suspicious of her. However, if she admitted to having the otherworld gate key, then all that awaited her was imprisonment and possibly death.

"Bayard, Caslain, hold those two down," Justice commanded.

Her eyes widening as Caslain placed his arms underneath her armpits, she tried to struggle out of his grip, but she'd already been pinned in place. Caslain was also much stronger than her. Beside her, Fellis was also in the same position, though she struggled and kicked a bit more. Sadly, they both knew that struggling was pointless. They were in a room with several powerful magicians and warriors.

Justice stepped up before her. His long wand went to her neck, pulling out the chain until the otherworld gate key popped free of her outfit.

"It's true," Justice muttered. "This is definitely the otherworld gate key."

"But that means…" Caslain's eyes widened. "You're the thief that I've been chasing all this time!"

"She must have summoned the beasts in an attempt to find out where the otherworld gate is," Abstinence accused.

"That's not it at all!" Enyo shouted. "In case you haven't realized, my magic is light magic. I can't use summoning magic."

"So you had an accomplice summon them for you." Abstinence waved off her attempts to defend herself.

"Enyo," Queen Alice said, and her gaze was both cold and conflicted. "Are you the one who stole the otherworld gate key while it was being transported?" Enyo said nothing. The queen closed her eyes, then opened them and yanked the otherworld gate key off Enyo's neck, ignoring Enyo's wince as the action rubbed her skin red. "Throw these two in the dungeon. We will decide on how to deal with them later."

Enyo thought about struggling. It wouldn't have been difficult to break out of Caslain's grip if she used magic. She decided not to, though, as doing so would have made her into more of a criminal and forced her to run. If she fought and escaped, she'd never be able to return to Avant Heim, and her dream of traveling to Jacob's world with him would disappear.

And so she said nothing as Caslain and Bayard escorted her out of the Great Hall.

It had been over a month since Jacob had been imprisoned, and in that time, not much had happened. Jacob spent most of his days exercising or meditating. The guards never said anything to him. He had the feeling they were afraid of him.

In the morning, his exercise consisted of push-ups and crunches. He did as many as he could, usually getting to a thousand before stopping for a break. Then he would rest and meditate for an hour before moving on to his next set of exercises.

The guards provided him with three meals a day. All the food was fairly delicious, considering he was a prisoner. Alice must have been the one responsible for that.

It was unfortunate that Durandal was no longer with him; he missed that sword. Since no one but he could even touch Durandal without being injured, it made sense that Durandal was probably locked away somewhere, cursing up a storm. His guess was the royal treasury. That was where all of the most valuable treasures were kept. Jacob wondered how difficult it had been to put a sword in there when it couldn't be touched.

I'll grab him when Enyo and I leave.

It was just as he thought this that the door to the dungeon opened. He frowned. The guards didn't change shift for another two hours, and Alice hadn't visited him since their last conversation.

Could it be Fellis again?

"All right, prisoners! Get in those cells!" someone shouted.

Jacob heard shuffling feet and a thud that sounded like someone being shoved forward. Letting his curiosity get the better of him, he walked over to his cell bars and looked out. He needed several seconds to comprehend what he was seeing. Enyo and Fellis were being shoved into separate jail cells next to his. The cell doors squealed closed and were locked shut with a click.

"Looks like you're going to have some company from now on, Hero," the knight who'd done the shoving said, spitting out the word "hero" as if it was a poison. He turned back around and muttered as he left. "I can't believe we once believed in this traitor."

Something had changed. That guard's disposition had been different from the last time they had spoken, which was respectful and apologetic. Just what had changed, he didn't know, but there were two people from whom he could gather information from.

"I'm guessing you two were found out?" he said.

"Astute observation," Fellis snarked. "What gave us away?"

"I'm just that amazing of a detective," Jacob replied before turning serious. "What happened?"

"Someone summoned several orthos to attack Avant Heim," Enyo said. She was sitting on her cell's cot, her knees drawn up to her chest. "We fought them off, but then Chastity came in and announced that we were the ones who summoned the orthos."

"But you're a light magic user," Jacob said, careful not to mention that she could use dark magic too. It wouldn't have mattered anyway, since dark magic couldn't summon anything, but he didn't want the guards overhearing that.

"They didn't care," Enyo muttered. "Once Chastity informed them that I had the otherworld gate key, everything else became irrelevant."

Jacob leaned his back against the wall and placed his hands on his face. "I see. So, someone found out that you were carrying the otherworld gate key. I'm assuming they confiscated it when they took you away."

"Yes."

"What I want to know is how Chastity found out," Fellis said. "It's not like we advertised the fact that she was carrying it, yet somehow, he found out in the middle of a combat situation."

Jacob wished he had an answer, but there was no way to figure that out. There could have been any number of methods. However, even as he thought them up, Jacob discarded practically all of them. Not even Queen Alice's magic, Foresight, had let her know that Enyo was carrying the otherworld gate key.

"What should we do?" Enyo asked.

"For now, let's wait," Jacob said. "Alice and the White Council will deliberate over what to do with you. Once we know their verdict, we can make our next decision."

Enyo said nothing. There wasn't a whole lot that she could say. She had stolen a royal treasure, the only key to the gate that was used to summon a hero. Only one possible outcome could come from this.

For stealing such valuable property, Enyo would be put to death.

INTERLUDE III - DARK PLAN HATCHED

They were in the White Council conference room again. However, this time they were not discussing the attack on Kindness and murder of two other White Council members; they were discussing what they should do with Enyo. As always, Alice sat at the technical head of the table, listening to the four remaining White Council members as they argued like a couple of children.

"We should sentence her to death and be done with it!" Abstinence shouted, slamming his hand onto the table as though doing so made his argument stronger.

"That sort of thinking is why nobody likes you," Kindness said.

"What was that?!"

"Queen Alice, I believe our first priority should be to find out what she was hoping to accomplish," Kindness said. "The fact that she offered to help us, that she saved my life when she didn't have to, should be enough to prove that Enyo is a good person."

"A good person?" Abstinence scoffed. "That woman is a member of the Dark Clan. There's not a single good person among them. They're all savages."

"That sort of unintelligent thinking is why everyone makes fun of you behind your back," Kindness retorted.

"Shut up!"

"This fighting is getting us nowhere," Alice said, interrupting them both. "I suggest you two calm down."

The debate thus far had been heated, with Abstinence calling for Enyo's death and Kindness defending her. Alice thought Kindness's defense of Enyo was because she was a foreigner. Unlike everyone else here, she'd not experienced the horrors of the war against the Dark Clan. She knew nothing of what they'd gone through.

Alice shifted in her seat. Despite the comfortable softness underneath her, her butt was getting numb. They'd been sitting there for at least two hours now. In that time, the only thing they'd done was argue, and she was getting sick of it.

"While I would normally agree with you, Kindness, do not forget that she had the otherworld gate key in her possession," Justice said. "Her rescue of you could have all been a ploy to get inside of Avant Heim."

"It could have, but I do not believe so," Kindness said. "Do not forget, there was no way for her to know who I was at the time she rescued me. It was the middle of the night when I was nearly killed, and she couldn't see my face."

"She might have been the one to sic those beasts on you to begin with," Justice said.

"What proof do you have that she did?" asked Kindness.

"What proof do you have that she didn't?" rebutted Justice.

Alice wanted to hang her head as she listened to these people bicker like children. She shifted again and looked at Listy, whose expression was carefully blank. Bayard and Caslain stood behind her, and while she couldn't see their expressions, she could well imagine them. They were probably as annoyed with this farce as she was.

"This sort of circular argument is getting us nowhere," Chastity said so suddenly that everyone stared at him in surprise. "Regardless of her reasons, it does not change the fact that she stole a royal treasure from Queen Alice, nor does it change that she is of the Dark Clan. A precedence has already been set for instances such as this, has it not? In which case, we have no choice but to go through with it."

Those who stole from the royal family were sentenced to death. It was a long-standing precedent set down by the first monarch of Terrasole. Not even nobility could escape from death if they stole something from the monarch.

Enyo, who was a Dark Clan member, had it even worse. She was their enemy. Quarter could not be shown. Mercy could not be given. To give mercy to a member of the Dark Clan was akin to allying oneself with them, and that was something they needed to avoid at all costs.

Alice closed her eyes. She didn't want to do this, but there was no other choice. To remain a a beacon of light and hope, to be viewed as an unbending leader to her people, a choice had to be made.

"I understand what everyone is saying. However, the ultimate decision still rests with me," she said, opening her eyes.

"That is indeed true, Your Majesty," Justice allowed. "The decision on what to do rests entirely on your shoulders. What do you think should be done?"

"For her crimes against the crown, Enyo shall be sentenced to death," Alice announced.

She had made the obvious choice, the right choice, the choice that any monarch would have made.

Even though doing so left her sick to her stomach.

✳✳✳

When the meeting ended, Chastity stood up with everyone else and filed out of the room. He took note of Kindness. She had rushed off in a seemingly random direction. He assumed she was going to sulk. Out of all the people there, she was the only one who tried to defend Enyo.

Justice and Abstinence were also leaving, though unlike the upset Kindness, they were exuding auras of smugness. He could practically feel their smirks as they congratulated each other on a job well done.

Chastity decided to leave the old men alone. Let them have their moment of arrogance. He would be the one standing on top in the end.

Since he already knew Avant Heim well, he wandered to the room that he had been given. It was located on the second floor of this wing.

Entering the room and locking the door behind him, Chastity took several steps into the luxurious chamber. His boots sank into the soft carpet. He looked at the few pieces of select artwork that hung from the walls with a frown. It was an atrocity that Queen Alice only gave him a room with these small comforts. She should have received him with her most luxurious room, preferably the same one that she used.

Of course, most of his attention was focused on the woman lying on his bed.

She was lying on her side. Her long, pale legs stretched out to the end of the bed, unhidden by the blanket that just barely covered her shapely hips. With her head resting against the palm of her hand, and her eyes absently scanning the pages of a book that lay in front of her, the woman looked both inhumanly alluring and intellectual. It created an aesthetic that somehow enhanced both aspects of her.

As the door closed behind him, she looked up, her hair swaying.

"Did everything go as planned?" she asked.

"Yes," Chastity said as he took off his boots, and then his shirt. He left his pants on as he crawled onto the bed. "It went exactly as you said it would."

She scooted back as he moved into the bed and laid down. The mattress lingered with her warmth and scent.

"Didn't I tell you? It is very easy to predict the outcome of all this. Now your position to the top has been secured."

Following her instructions, Chastity had created a crack in the barrier surrounding Avant Heim, which had allowed her into the castle unimpeded. She'd then destroyed the barrier from the inside out and set loose several orthos. While the orthos had attacked, he'd run off, presumably to draw their attention. What he'd actually been doing was meeting up with her.

She'd informed him about Enyo, who she was, and how she was the thief they'd been looking for. It had been easy to place the blame for the orthos on Enyo once everyone learned that she was in possession of the otherworld gate key. They hadn't even bothered questioning her.

Chastity felt goosebumps rise as the woman drew circles on his chest. "Yes. Now all that is left to do is use the lack of White Council members to cement my position."

"Indeed," she said, a smile curling her lips.

✳✳✳

Many years ago, Kindness had lived in a world filled with war. People died every day, either because someone had killed them, they'd died from famine and disease, or they simply lost the will to live. Being one of the few people in her country with an aptitude for magic, her kingdom had tried to turn her into a weapon.

It had been many years since she'd thought about the life she left behind. Thanks to her mentor, who'd been humane and kind, she'd escaped from that life. After arriving in Terrasole, she had made a name for herself by helping people with magic. She would travel the country, aiding everyone who needed it. Her aptitude for magic had eventually caught the eye of the Royal Family. It had been the former king himself who'd requested that she become a member of his magicians. Kindness had agreed, but only if he promised not to use her powers to kill.

Having grown up in a place where death and lawlessness were common, Kindness had a strong sense of justice and a hatred of violence. She knew when something wrong was being committed upon someone by another. Thanks to her kindness, she also had trouble standing aside and letting it happen.

That was why she had snuck out of her bedroom in the middle of the night and traveled to the dungeon. Two knights stood guard at the door. Kindness frowned. She didn't want to kill them, which meant...

"Circum. Globus."

Kindness felt a small tug on her navel as the words helped channel her magic. Two spheres coalesced before her, perfectly round, gleaming with the brightness of metal. It wasn't metal, however, but energy given shape and changed into the same consistency of metal. It looked like metal, acted like metal, but it wasn't really metal. This was her magic: Conjure.

Conjure could create any object that existed, so long as Kindness had the imagination and energy to create it. Of course, the more complicated objects couldn't be conjured unless she had knowledge of how they worked. That said, conjuring simple objects like these spheres was easier than breathing.

The two spheres hovered in the air for but a second, and then they shot forward, striking the two guards in the neck, between the junctions protected by armor. Her attacks had been precise. The guards dropped like sacks of bricks.

With her path clear, Kindness entered the dungeon tower and walked down. Voices reached her from below. They were loud and raucous... and slurred. She really hoped the guards weren't drunk.

She reached the door. It was old and rickety, and it squealed when she opened it a crack. Peering inside, Kindness, for a moment, wondered if she'd somehow been transported to another world, one in which strange and delusional happenings were commonplace. It was the only way to explain what she was seeing.

The guards were dancing, merrily, gaily, as if they'd gone on an all-night drinking spree.

They were also doing so on the table.

They were also naked.

Standing outside of their cells, clapping in time to the guards' dancing, Enyo, Fellis, and someone she recognized as the Hero Jacob, all seemed to be enjoying themselves a good deal. At the very least, Fellis had an amused grin.

She opened the door fully and stepped in, shutting the door behind her with a solid thump.

"What are you all doing?"

Enyo, Fellis, and Jacob stopped clapping to look at her. The guards were still dancing, however.

"We're watching these two make fools out of themselves," Fellis answered.

"Yes, I can see that," Kindness said dryly. "Let me rephrase that question. How did this happen?"

Fellis's eyes were alight as she spoke. "Well, you see, I had previously come down this way to speak with Jacob the other night, and these guards were the ones who'd previously fallen sway to my magic. I already them under my mind control, so I thought to myself, 'Why not have a little fun?'"

After staring at Fellis and her unrepentant grin for several more seconds, Kindness looked at Enyo. "Why didn't you stop her?"

"I could have, but I was bored," Enyo admitted with a shrug.

Kindness stared at Enyo some more, and then looked at Jacob. He shrugged. "If you can't beat them, join them."

There was something unnatural about this situation. For the life of her, Kindness couldn't figure out what. It was probably because of the headache thinking about this gave her, and since it was giving her such a massive headache, she decided not to think about it anymore.

"I suppose now is not the time for us to speak about this matter," Kindness said. "Since you are already outside of your cells, this should make things simpler. Listen, Queen Alice has determined that Enyo is going to be sentenced to death. You have to escape."

Her words sobered the trio up. Their expressions became grave, their countenance shifted, the very air around them seemed to become denser. It felt like when a feral animal found themselves trapped by a hunter and was preparing to attack. She supposed she couldn't blame them.

"I... suppose that is only natural," Enyo admitted at last. "I did steal the otherworld gate key, and I'm of the Dark Clan. Our kind doesn't exactly get along with humans."

"Speaking of the otherworld gate key, why did you steal it?" Kindness asked.

Enyo looked at Jacob, who she seemed to hold a silent conversation with. For whatever reason, Kindness felt mildly uncomfortable as she watched them speak without words. It felt like she was looking into a private conversation between lovers.

"Because I want to send Jacob back to his world," Enyo said at last. "Not just that, but I would like to start a new life with Jacob in his world."

Even though her answer had been kind of expected, it still shocked Kindness. Even though she was surprised, it really did make a lot of sense. Why else would someone seek to claim the otherworld gate key if not to travel to another world?

"You do know that there is a chance you won't be able to go with Jacob," Kindness said. "It has been a well-documented fact that people from our world cannot travel through the otherworld gate."

"That may be so," Jacob started, "but we're hoping that she'll be able to travel through it if I am with her."

"And if she can't?"

"Then we'll find another way to reach my world," Jacob said, his eyes burning with determination. "After everything that's happened between us, I'm not leaving Enyo behind."

"Jacob…"

Kindness coughed several times when Enyo placed a hand over Jacob's. She was not at all comfortable with their intimate display. And speaking of, she wondered what was happening between these two. Were they lovers? How in the goddess's name had that happened?

"In any case, you three should take this opportunity to leave. Come tomorrow morning, Enyo will be dragged out of this cell and put to death. That is why you should go now."

"You bring up a good point," Fellis said, standing up. "We were staying here because we had hope that this situation might turn around at some point, but if we're not even getting a chance to plead our case, then there isn't much we can do but leave."

"What will happen to you?" Enyo asked.

Kindness smiled. Even though she was the one who's life was in jeopardy, Enyo still worried about her. It was moments like this, more than anything else, that let Kindness know she was making the right choice.

"Do not worry about me," Kindness said. "I'm not the one with a death sentence on her head."

To that, all Enyo could say was, "Touché."

CHAPTER 5 - ESCAPE
FROM ALYSSIUM

Since they had decided to escape, he, Enyo, and Fellis, followed Kindness as she led them out of the dungeon. They moved swiftly across the courtyard, traveled through the castle, and evaded detection from the guards. As they moved, Jacob couldn't help but wonder about something.

What will Alice do when she finds the guards still dancing inside of the dungeon?

A thought for another time.

It didn't take long to reach the castle gates. Fellis had used her Mind Manipulation magic to make the guards forget they were there. Kindness had given her a strange look, but fortunately, she seemed to have realized that Fellis wasn't the type to just manipulate people on a whim—unless it was for a prank.

Like making guards dance naked on the table.

Since they were already inside of Avant Heim, they needn't worry about the barrier. Kindness opened the large gate, a massive structure of gleaming silver and gold, and then closed it when Enyo, Fellis, and he exited.

"I'll be returning to my room now," Kindness said. "Thank you again for saving me when you did. I hope... I hope you manage to find happiness in this world if you can't travel to Jacob's."

"Thank you very much," Enyo said. "Stay safe."

"Come on." Jacob grabbed Enyo's hand and gave it a gentle tug. "We'd better get a move on. The sooner we leave the city, the better."

"Right."

Jacob took Enyo and Fellis down the steps that would lead into the noble district. He looked behind them. Kindness was no longer there, having likely disappeared back into the castle.

Ever since the three White Council members were murdered, the soldiers stationed in Alyssium had been on constant guard duty. Soldiers patrolled the streets at night in squads of three. Jacob, who knew Alyssium better than Fellis and Enyo did, guided them along the routes that would have the least amount of guards.

The noble district had the largest number of guards. Jacob avoided them by traveling through parks and only straying into streets when there was no other option. Several times, they ran into a patrol, but each time that happened, he and Ellis would subdue two of them while Fellis used her Mind Manipulation to control the first one, and then ensnare the others, making them forget that they ever saw the three of them.

Before long, they had traveled down the large stone steps that led to the Market District.

"How long will it take to reach the gates?" asked Fellis.

"That depends on how many guards we have to evade," Jacob said. "As a straight shot, it's only about an hour, but we're not going straight for the gate. I'd say... maybe two or three hours—five at the most."

"Then let's hurry," Enyo suggested.

Jacob moved swiftly down the road. Up ahead, three guards were patrolling. The fairy lamps were on, providing enough illumination to spot them. They were coming this way. Fortunately, they didn't seem to have noticed him, Enyo, or Fellis yet. Knowing better than to remain on the road, he darted into an alley, the other two following close behind.

"There's a side street up ahead," he told them. "It'll take us to a place where we can get onto the roofs. We'll travel along the roofs for a while and get down when we're closer to the gate."

"Is it wise to travel the roofs?" asked Fellis. "What about drake patrols?"

Jacob shook his head. "They don't use drakes for patrol unless they're actively searching for someone. Right now, everyone is just on guard. We won't need to worry about drakes."

Even as he said this, Jacob's danger sense went out of control as he sensed the air shift above them. Looking up, he barely had a second to shove Fellis and Enyo away before a dark object slammed into him. Stifling his scream of pain, he channeled energy into his arms, legs, and torso as he shoved the object off.

The "thing" was actually a creature. It was similar to an orthos in that it had four legs, a long tail, and bristling fur, but that was where the similarities came to an end. Three vicious muzzles barked at him. Six glowing red eyes gazed at him with an insatiable hunger as if he was their next meal. Drool dripped from its three mouths, falling to the road and sizzling as it melted right through them. It pawed at the ground. Gouges appeared in the road.

"Oh, great," Jacob muttered. "A Cerberus."

Cerberus were three-headed dogs that were said to have originally been guardians of the underworld. He didn't know where that particular legend had come from, but Jacob did know that they were used to guard ancient treasures. He'd fought them on a number of occasions. Mostly, he found them inside of dungeons and caverns. They were strong, fast, intelligent, and damn near impervious to most attacks.

"Jacob," Enyo said as she stared at the large creature with eyes that were reminiscent to a rodent that had been trapped by a cat. "What should we do?"

"What do you mean what should we do?" Jacob asked back. "Isn't that obvious? We run!"

The cerberus howled as it leapt at him. Jacob reinforced himself with Linked Energy Manipulation and slammed a fist into the ground. A giant chunk of road jutted into the air, which the cerberus slammed into face first—well, one of its faces did. The other two snapped at the chunk and crushed it in their jaws.

Not wasting any time, Jacob followed through with a devastating kick that launched the creature into the air.

"Let's go!" Jacob shouted.

They raced through the alley and burst into the side street that he'd been talking about before they were attacked. Because of the cerberus, Jacob decided not to travel via the roofs. If it found them, it would follow them, and if it followed them... well, he didn't want to imagine the kind of damage it would do to the roofs.

Loud howling echoed behind them. Jacob would have groaned if he wasn't so busy running. The unmistakable thudding of paws hitting pavement resounded with a touch of ominousness. If he turned his head, Jacob knew that he'd see the cerberus bounding toward them.

"It's chasing us!" Enyo shouted.

"I know that!" Jacob yelled back.

"What should we do?" asked Fellis.

Jacob didn't have long to think about their next move; the cerberus's howling was getting closer. He came up with a decision that would either work brilliantly or end up with them being worse off than before.

"Follow me!" he commanded.

They vacated the side street with an immediate right turn. The cerberus, which had been moving way too fast for such a quick turn, skidded along the ground and slid right past the alley they'd run into. Jacob didn't stick around. He knew this move would only give them an extra second or two at most.

He took another turn, left this time, and continued running until the next turn, which he also took. Again and again, he took as many twists and turns as possible. No matter how many turns he took, the cerberus stayed close behind them. He could hear its heavy breathing, its grunts and its growls, and the sound of its feet gouging out chunks of the cobblestone roads. Given that it had an amazing sense of smell, there was no way they could lose it.

It was a good thing that he wasn't trying to lose it.

"Get ready to scream for help," Jacob told the two.

"W-what?" Enyo asked.

"Three. Two. One. Scream!"

Despite clearly not understanding why he asked this of them, they screamed anyway, shouting *"HEELLLPPP!!!"* at the top of their lungs as they burst out of the alley. Two guard patrols who'd been just passing each other on the street stopped. They looked at the three of them, their expressions startled. Those gawking faces soon turned into outright fear as the cerberus suddenly leapt out from the alley. However, even afraid, they were still knights, and their job was to protect the innocent.

They charged at the cerberus and started attacking it. The cerberus howled as it tried to swat the knights out of its way, but even if they weren't trained to slay monsters, Terrasole's knights were still excellent fighters. They wove around the cerberus's giant paws as it swiped at them. Each attack caused it to change targets, but it was being attacked from so many different directions that it couldn't figure out who to attack first. It didn't help that all three of its heads wanted to attack a different enemy.

It was the cerberus's one weakness.

"Let's hurry up and leave," Jacob said as he raced down the street.

They were already near the gate. It loomed before them, a massive archway composed of bricks. Guards patrolled the top while several more stood in front of the gargantuan metal gates. Fairy lights situated on the walls illuminated the area, allowing him to see the doorway that led inside of the wall. Jacob knew there would be a lever inside.

"You two take out the guards in front of the gate. I'll take out the ones inside, open the gate, and then we can make our escape."

"That is a plan I can get behind," Fellis said. "You'd better be quick, though. There's no telling how long those knights can keep that cerberus occupied."

"I know."

They split up; Jacob rushed for the door while Enyo and Fellis charged the guards. He heard shouting, which was quickly followed by the clashing of weapons, as he busted the door in and rushed inside.

"What the—who are you?!" a guard shouted. He'd apparently had the misfortune of walking down the hall when Jacob was in a hurry.

Jacob didn't even bother answering that question. He slammed a reinforced fist into the guard's chest, breaking the plate armor and sending the knight crashing to the ground. To keep the guard down, he'd also sent a good dose of energy into the man, scrambling his nervous system.

Rushing past the downed guard, Jacob traveled up a set of stairs, down a hall, and entered a large room. The lever was in the room. So was another guard. Jacob didn't even give the guard time to shout before he rushed forward, jammed his elbow into her throat, and then knocked her upside the head. The guard crumpled to the floor, allowing Jacob to pull the lever.

The wall shook as the sound of metal cranking echoed around him. Jacob raced back outside to find that Enyo and Fellis had already taken care of their guards. Of course, since they hadn't been subtle, a lot of the guards up top were yelling, and several were already running to get down. Also, and Jacob almost swore when he noticed this, but the cerberus was bounding toward them again, howling like a ravenous beast who'd just spotted its next meal.

It seems the knights couldn't keep it occupied for long. Damn.

"I think we've overstayed our welcome," Enyo said.

"Then let's get going," Jacob responded.

With the cerberus still chasing them, the guards shouting, and their hearts pounding in their chests, Enyo, Jacob, and Fellis left Alyssium behind.

***

Alyssium was a gorgeous place, not just its city, which was renowned for its cleanliness and beautiful gardens. The surrounding forests that covered the area around Alyssium was just as gorgeous. Thick trees held a vibrant glow as the morning sun struck them, soft grass glistened with morning dew, and the sound of songbirds singing their tune would have normally made all who heard it feel at peace.

Except normally there wasn't a large dog with three heads chasing people through the forest.

Jacob didn't know how far they'd run. It wasn't like he'd been keeping track of their pace, but they had to have been at least several kilometers from Alyssium by now. He felt like they'd been running for hours, and while that was fine with him, Enyo and Fellis looked ready drop.

"We're making our stand here," Jacob announced.

"What?" Enyo gasped. Even exhausted and making nasally rasps as she ran, she still had it in her to look at him with a wide-eyed expression. "You've got to be kidding me."

"I'm not kidding you. We can't outrun this cerberus forever. We have to face it now before we run out of energy."

"Ugh." Fellis grimaced. "I think I ran out of that several hours ago."

"Whatever. Look, if you two could each keep one of its heads occupied, I can take care of the rest."

Behind them, the cerberus howled as it slammed into and smashed apart several trees. Fellis, who'd looked back and saw the dog's steaming slobber eat through wood and rock alike, grimaced, and looked back at him.

"You're asking for a mighty tall order."

"It's either that or we all die," Jacob said.

Another grimace. "Point taken."

"I'll take... the left..." Enyo rasped, pulling out a pair of daggers she must have stolen from a guard.

"Then... I guess I've got right."

Enyo and Fellis stopped running and turned around. The cerberus was literally right behind them. Enyo muttered under her breath and sent a white orb of light at it. The orb struck its left head, igniting like an exploding star.

Cerberus were magically resistant. Magical resistance was a term used to describe creatures or people who magic didn't work on very well. A cerberus's thick hide protected it from all but the most powerful attacks. Even for someone like Enyo, who's three-word chants were powerful enough to destroy toad demons, it would take at least a twelve-word chant to build up enough power to damage a cerberus, never mind killing it.

That said, blinding it was another matter entirely.

As the cerberus head howled in shock and rage, Fellis lashed out with her whip, striking the rightmost cerberus head in the face. She got lucky and gouged its left eye. Blood spurted from the wound. The creature roared as it jerked back.

Racing forward, Enyo struck the creature in the face with her dagger, imbued with the magical essence of Darkness. Even with her weapon imbued with magic, the blade still only left a scratch. Just like Jacob had suspected, this cerberus, like all the others, was strong against physical attacks and magic. Only a really strong spell would be enough to slay something like this, and Enyo didn't have any time to chant a long spell.

Jacob knew that he needed to deal with this thing in one blow. Cerberus were tenacious. They'd keep attacking until they were mulch, no matter how much pain they were in or what limbs were missing. It was better for both him and the cerberus if it died quickly.

Channeling energy through every part of his body, Jacob enhanced himself until his energy burst from his pores. It was a physical aura shaped like a flame. He could feel it rushing through him like a typhoon.

His body tore. He could practically hear the sound of his muscles tearing under the strain. He hadn't even used this much power during his fight with Lust because he was still so out of shape. He was going to be a wreck after this.

Once we leave this place, I'm going to start training again.

"Move out of the way, you two!" he shouted.

Enyo and Fellis took that as their cue and leapt aside. The two cerberus heads they'd been fighting tried to go off in separate directions. This left the middle head wide open, and it was that head that Jacob aimed for.

Before the cerberus could see him, he appeared in front of it, throwing out his left fist and smashing it into the middle head. Then he unleashed all the stored-up energy in his body. It burst from his knuckles like a massive cone of destructive force. The cerberus was engulfed in the conical beam of energy. The wind howled, the air was rent, the cerberus's yowling was overpowered by the roar of his attack, and through it all, Jacob gritted his teeth as the skin on his knuckles was burnt off.

When the energy petered out, the cerberus was gone—along with about fifty meters worth of forest.

Fellis whistled. "That was impressive, but don't you think you went a little overboard?"

Wiping the sweat from his head, Jacob disagreed. "No. A cerberus is one of the strongest beasts around. The best way to deal with one is in a single, decisive blow." He looked back at the giant trench and sighed. "That said, I might have used a bit too much power back there. I was panicked, so I didn't have good control over my energy."

"I think that was awesome," Enyo admitted.

Jacob grinned. "Well, thank you."

"What should we do now?" asked Fellis.

"Leave," Jacob said bluntly. "That last attack of mine is bound to have been noticed by Alyssium. Even if they aren't aware of our escape, they'll at least send someone to check this place out."

"Where should we go?" Enyo asked. "I'm not even sure where we are."

"Don't worry." Jacob sent her a reassuring smile. "I know where we are. We're in the northern quadrant of the forest. If we travel about twenty kilometers north, we'll eventually hit the sea."

At the mention of the sea, Enyo's eyes sparkled. "I've never been to the sea before."

"You probably won't be able to for a while yet," Jacob said apologetically. "While that will be our next destination, we need to find a place to rest first."

"Tired after that last attack?" Fellis teased.

"I think we're all tired," Jacob countered.

"I second that," Enyo agreed. "I could do with a nap right about now."

"See that? Enyo agrees with me."

"Hey, I never said I disagreed." Fellis shrugged. "I'm just saying."

Journeying through the forest was, fortunately, easier than fighting a giant three-headed dog. Jacob took the lead. He walked through the trees, placing his hands on them as if somehow communing with nature. He wasn't, of course. Jacob couldn't talk to trees, but he'd played in these forests many times before going off on his journey, and he could tell where they were based on the feel of the bark.

They eventually came upon a large waterfall connected to a lake. The blue waters were clear as crystal—so clear it was possible to see the bottom, along with the fish and other water animals that made the lake their home. Glades of tall grass jutted from the water, swaying in the breeze, and an array of colorful flowers bloomed near the edge.

"Oh, wow," Enyo muttered. "It's so gorgeous."

"Isn't it?" Jacob said with a smile. "I stumbled upon this place when I was twelve. Anyway, there's a cave behind that waterfall. It should serve as adequate shelter from search parties."

There was, indeed, a cave behind the waterfall. It was surprisingly large, almost tunnel-like in how far back it went. The rock walls were sturdy, if uneven. Water dripped from the ceiling and ran between cracks in the walls. Their feet splashed against puddles on the floor.

Since they were trying to avoid detection, Jacob led them all the way to the back. It was a lot drier in the back as well.

Because of their hasty exit, they didn't have much in the way of supplies, or indeed, any supplies to speak of. Jacob had to find twigs and branches and used old-fashioned methods to light a fire. He also caught some fish and grilled them over the fire so they'd have something to eat.

Everyone decided to get some rest after their light meal. Fellis laid down on her side and fell asleep almost immediately. Jacob laid on his back several meters from Fellis and also tried to get some sleep. It proved impossible, not because he wasn't tired—he was—but because he knew that Enyo was still awake.

He opened his eyes a crack and glanced at Enyo, who sat in front of the fire with her knees drawn up to her chest. Sighing, he realized that he wasn't going to be able to sleep with her like that. He was too worried.

Jacob stood up and wandered over to the fire, sitting down next to her and feeding the fire some more wood. He didn't say anything. Instead, he waited for Enyo to speak, which she did, eventually.

"You know, I... even though I expressed a lot of confidence in you when we were separated, I was really worried about you," Enyo admitted. "It was even harder when I heard you'd been imprisoned. If it wasn't for the confidence that I have in you, I would've worried myself to death."

"I'm sorry for worrying you," Jacob said. "I hadn't meant to let myself be captured like that. Lust proved to be a stronger opponent than I imagined."

"Lust? You mean that woman from the Dark Council?"

"That's the one. It seems I underestimated her a great deal. She might not have your old man's power, but her experience was able to easily counter my own strength. To be honest, I'm kind of ashamed about how handily she defeated me."

"I can't believe she defeated you, either." Enyo wrapped her arms around herself. "I've grown up hearing stories about the Dark Council, about their power and their cunning. Even though I knew they were strong, I still never imagined they could be strong enough to beat you."

Jacob thought back to his battle against Lust. It was true that he'd been defeated, but he felt like part of the reason was because he'd been holding back. They had been fighting in the middle of a human city, so it wasn't like he could have gone all out, lest he wanted to demolish the entire city and kill its people, which he didn't want. The last thing he wanted was more death on his hands.

However, there was also the matter of experience. His battle with Lust had shown that she knew more about combat than he did, that she had experienced more than him. Her tactics, her deception, the way she used her powers to trick him and then hit him from behind, it all denoted to one irrepressible fact: Lust was simply a better and more cunning tactician than he was.

"I'm sorry, Jacob," Enyo said suddenly.

"Huh?" Jacob glanced at her. "What are you sorry for?"

"For everything," Enyo admitted. "I dragged you all this way with me, promised to send you back to your world, and even decided that I was going to go with you, but I couldn't keep my promise to you. I was found out and the otherworld gate key was taken back. I don't even know if I can keep my promise to return you to your world now."

Placing a hand against his chest, Jacob wondered if the warmth he felt was due to her words or what her words meant. She was more worried about keeping her promise to him than she was about herself. It had been so long since someone had put him first. He'd forgotten what it felt like.

He scooted a little bit closer, close enough that their shoulders were touching. "You know, I don't really think I would mind staying in this world if it meant being with you."

"W-what?"

Jacob smiled at her wide-eyed expression. "Before you appeared in front of me, my life was pointless, dull, and monochrome. It had no meaning beyond living to see the next day. You changed that. Since meeting you, I've remembered what it was like to have companions and people you trust to watch your back. I've been able to smile and laugh. I've been having fun. All of that is thanks to you."

Enyo's face lit up in a fetching blush. She looked away, as if doing so would somehow hide the redness of her cheeks.

"I-I didn't do much."

"You did enough," Jacob countered. He placed a hand on her cheek and turned her head around so she was facing him again. "I want you to know that I'm very grateful to you. Not just that, but I'm glad you showed up in my bar all those months ago."

"O-oh…" Enyo wasn't able to turn her head because of his hand, so she shifted her eyes away from his face. "Y-you're welcome."

"Enyo, now that you've gotten a chance to know me, do you still love me?" he asked. Enyo looked back at him. "I know that you had feelings for the hero known as Jacob Stone, but now that you know he's just a normal person who abandoned his duties because he felt betrayed, how do you feel about him?"

No answer was forthcoming at first. After another moment, however, Enyo, her cheeks still lit up like fireworks at a festival, said, "My feelings haven't changed… no, if anything, my feelings for you have only… they've become stronger. When I was younger, I only loved Jacob because of the stories I'd heard, because you were a hero, but now that I've gotten to know the real you... w-well, I think the real Jacob is a lot better than the stories I've been told."

"Is that so?"

"Hm."

Jacob had been reluctant to let himself grow to love this young woman at first, even after finding out about her crush on him. There hadn't been time, he'd told himself. They were on a journey and couldn't afford to let themselves get distracted, he would argue with himself. Yet the longer he spent in her presence, the fonder he became of her. And after they were torn apart, his fondness for her had become even stronger. It had grown to the point where Jacob felt like he could be happy even if he didn't return home, so long as he could remain with her.

What had really made him realize his feelings was when he and Enyo had been separated. While he'd kept himself occupied in prison, not a day had gone by when he hadn't thought about Enyo, when he hadn't wondered if she was safe. The idea that she might be in trouble and he didn't know it had made his chest ache. That, more than anything, had confirmed the feelings that he'd been doing his best to put off.

"In that case, I believe there is something important that I need to tell you," Jacob confessed as he leaned down until their foreheads were touching.

Enyo's pink eyes were like rounded plates. Her cheeks, caressed with a lovely shade of pink, complemented by her snowy skin and pink hair. From the moment they had met, Jacob had thought she was beautiful. However, it was moments like this that made her appear truly enchanting.

"What do you want to tell me?" asked Enyo, her voice a mere whisper.

"I wanted to let you know that I love you, too," he said before leaning down the rest of the way and pressing his lips to hers.

Enyo went stock still for a moment as if she'd been zapped by lightning. Yet the moment soon passed, and she responded to the kiss with the same eagerness she had when fighting—only less violent.

Her arms went around his neck, and her head tilted up to better access his lips.

As the kiss continued, Jacob decided right then and there that even if he never saw his home again, he would be okay.

There were some people in this world who he didn't want to live without.

***

Enyo frowned as the boat that she was on rocked and swayed. She didn't particularly like the motions. It didn't help that she was blindfolded. For whatever reason, having a blindfold covering her while the boat rocked and swayed, creaked and groaned, made her sick to her stomach. Why did they even have to put this thing on her anyway? She was in a holding cell. It wasn't like she could actually see where they were going.

They probably thought it would be amusing. Damn pirates.

About a month ago, a group of pirates had shown up around the Njord Peninsula. They'd kidnapped several young women from various villages across the peninsula, but none of the locals had been able to do anything. That was why she was there. Her job was to locate the pirate stronghold.

Of course, that meant getting herself captured.

She leaned against the wall. Her hands had been tied behind her back, but that didn't concern her overly much. It would be a simple matter to break her bonds. A single word incantation would be enough to sever the ropes tying her down.

I wonder how far out at sea we are?

It had probably been around a day since she'd allowed herself to be kidnapped. None of the pirates had tried anything yet... well, one person had gotten a little frisky, but that man was now missing a hand. She knew that she needed to act the part of a helpless woman, but there was no way she'd allow some grubby man with dirty hands to fondle her.

The creaking of the door opening made Enyo turn her head. Still acting the part of a scared young woman, she huddled near the corner of the holding cell. The person who walked in chuckled.

"P-please don't hurt me," Enyo begged, making her voice as high pitched as possible.

"Don't ye worry, lass. Me boys and I ain't gonna hurt ye. Yer far too valuable fer that," the man said in a heavily accented voice. She couldn't place his accent, but she didn't think he was from Terrasole. "Our, ahem, customers like it when the merchandise we sell is unsullied."

It took a lot of effort to remain in character, especially since all she wanted to do was throw this man out of a window. Still, she knew that she couldn't afford to lose her cool. A lot of young women were depending on her.

Jacob, I hope you're having a more pleasant time than I am.

✳✳✳

Jacob wasn't having a pleasant time. At all. The problem was that he just didn't like boats. They rocked and wobbled and were altogether unpleasant. It didn't help that his boat was tiny. He could feel every motion made, and it was making him sick.

Up ahead, the boat that Enyo was on could be seen as a small speck in the distance. The plan was for him to follow from a distance, while Enyo infiltrated them by pretending to be taken captive. They would both attack once they knew the location of the captured women.

Unfortunately, the ship had been traveling all day and showed no sign of stopping.

Putting a telescope to his eye, Jacob watched the ship as it sailed into what appeared to be an archipelago. He removed the telescope and began rowing again. His muscles burst with energy as he used Linked Energy Manipulation to enhance them, which consequently caused the boat that he was in to speed across the water's surface.

He followed the ship into the archipelago. Jacob was careful to stay outside of any potential observer's sights, sticking to the ship's blind spots where sailors didn't bother looking because who would be stupid enough to follow a ship that large unless they were in a ship that was just as large and had weapons to defend themselves with.

This allowed him to move without being noticed, and it allowed him to stay in sight of the ship as it sailed into the large entrance of a cave.

This must be their hideout.

Now all he needed to do was sneak inside, wait for Enyo to start the party, and then join the fray.

Simple.

***

Enyo was grateful when the boat finally stopped. Not only did it mean she wouldn't feel so queasy, but it also meant they had docked. Hopefully, this meant she would be able to end this charade soon.

The door creaked open and footsteps echoed around the room. "A'ight, Missy. It's time ye came with me!"

A filthy hand grabbed her arm. Enyo was hauled to her feet. Her blindfold was removed, and then shoved forward, toward where she knew was the door. With her hands tied behind her back, a pirate shoving her along, and her weapons with Jacob, she strode forward, leaving the holding cell and making for the stairs.

As she stepped onto the deck, the wooden planks creaked beneath her feet. She turned her head, looking up at the mast, which had a blank flag that was currently slack. It showed no symbol, denoting that it had no affiliation with any country. All around her, men stopped what they'd been doing as she walked by at sword point. They catcalled and howled, made degrading remarks, and wolf-whistled. She ignored them. Once Jacob came with her daggers, these jerks were getting an enema, Enyo style.

The boarding plank was already attached to the dock. The pirate behind her, a grizzled old man with a missing hand, stained teeth, and a haggard face, pushed her down the boarding plank. She would have kicked him already, but she contained herself. She needed to find the women who'd been kidnapped. Then she could kick ass.

Her footsteps and those of the pirate's echoed ominously inside of the vast cavern. The sound of water splashing against the ship and rock faces accompanied the rhythm of her feet. Enyo felt a mild moment of discomfort as she stepped on the dock, which groaned underneath her weight.

"Keep going, miss," the pirate behind her said, using the word "miss" like it was a personal insult.

Enyo said nothing as she was led deeper into the cavern. There appeared to be many intersecting passages in this cave, and the route that she was forced to take was winding and twisted, sort of like the people who'd kidnapped her.

Upon reaching a rickety old door, the pirate opened it and shoved her inside. "Yer gonna be stayin' in there until we're ready to sell ye off," he said before slamming the door shut.

"Prig," Enyo muttered under her breath as she straightened up.

Blinking several times to let her eyes adjust, Enyo gazed at the many frightened and tear-streaked faces that greeted her. They were the women who'd been kidnapped. They were all huddled against the wall, bound at the wrists like her. She frowned for a moment, but then put on a reassuring smile.

"Excuse me," she called out, "but do any of you know if there are any other captives being held somewhere else?"

No one spoke at first. She had the strangest feeling that they were confused. They looked at each other, as if silently asking the people around them what she was talking about. However, one brave girl, who couldn't have been older than fourteen years of age, stepped up.

"There is one other person," she said. "My friend Mari. She spoke out and wouldn't listen to the people who kidnapped us. They took her away somewhere."

"But you don't know where?" Enyo asked. The girl shook her head. "Okay, then. Listen up, everyone! I'm getting all of you out of here!"

"How do you plan to do that?" someone asked.

"Yeah, you're a captive just like us!" another shouted.

Muttering a quick spell under her breath, feeling a tug on her navel, Enyo created a black flame in her hands, which ate the rope binding her. She showed her now-free arms to the women, who gawked at her like they'd just witnessed a miracle, and then she said,

"I'm not a captive. I came here specifically to rescue all of you. Now, follow me and try to be quiet, okay?"

The group of women still seemed to be in shock. However, they followed her anyway, as she broke the ropes binding them and led them out of the room.

Enyo was thankful for her good memory, or she would have never been able to memorize the route that she had taken to get there. They reached the end of the tunnel after numerous twists and turns.

The pirates were all offloading cargo, with some carrying large barrels while others offloaded giant boxes. It seemed women weren't all they stole. She would've wondered what all that stuff was, but she didn't really care.

"How are we going to escape from this place?" one of the women asked.

Enyo turned her head to grin at the person. "You'll see."

Turning back, Enyo took a moment to calm herself. Slowly, as if in a trance, she started to chant.

"Creperum. Ignis. Incendo. Exitium. Eversio. Ruina. Vena. Displodo. Abolesco. Flamen."

Enyo felt the tug on her navel as magic was pulled from her reserves. She held her hands about a dozen centimeters apart. Dark streaks of energy coalesced between her hands, gathering until it had formed a tiny ball about the size of a golden coin. Taking a calming breath, Enyo stepped out from behind the cover, and launched the sphere at the ship.

The results were devastating.

The sphere of compressed dark flames struck the side of the ship like the fist of an angry god. It exploded against the hull, busting straight through one side and going out the other side. Then came the turbulent winds. It was like watching a tornado appear sideways. The ship broke apart as a large vortex tore through the space. Everything was sucked inside—wood, water, people. A massive trench was created in the water as it was split.

Enyo bit her lower lip. "I think I might have used too much magic."

She thought about that for a moment, but then she shrugged. These people were pirates. What did she care of she annihilated their stuff?

"Stay right here," she said to the women, all of whom were gawking at her. "My boyfriend should be coming in just a minute. We'll get you out of here soon."

***

Jacob was liberally tossed out of his boat when a massive cyclone rushed out from the cave and capsized him. He yelped as he flipped through the air. Channeling energy into his feet, he struck the water's surface with a massive splash.

Standing on the water, Jacob looked at the cavern. There was a large vortex traveling out of it. It ripped through the water, a tornado traveling horizontally, creating massive waves that rocked the water he stood on, even though he was several meters away.

"That girl..." He pressed a hand to his face. "She's going overboard again."

Withholding a sigh, he raced across the water's surface, sending a constant stream of energy to the bottom of his feet in order to stay afloat. Jacob reached the cavern in record time. Glancing inside, he saw that much of the surrounding waters had been disturbed—no surprise there. Enyo was on the cavern floor near a large cave entrance.

She was also fighting barehanded against what appeared to be several dozen pirates.

Not wasting another second, Jacob bent his knees, channeled energy through his lower body, and shot forward. The water roared underneath him as it turned into a wave. Launched into the air, he oriented his feet until they were pointed at one of the pirates fighting against Enyo. His feet slammed into that person's back. The pirate went flying, slammed into the cavern wall, and there he remained, embedded in the rock.

"Enyo!" Jacob shouted as he reached behind him, pulled out her daggers, and tossed them to her.

She caught the daggers. This distracted her from the pirates that she was fighting. Fortunately, Jacob was paying attention for her and sent a massive wave of blue energy that slammed into the pirates like a rampaging elephanté.

"Thanks!" Enyo said as she finally attached the sheaths to her thighs. She pulled out her daggers and, raising them in a crossguard, blocked a sword strike that would have split open her head. Then she kicked the pirate who'd attacked her in the nuts. As his scream reached several octaves higher than normal, her daggers became engulfed in magic; one was a dark flame and the other a bright, divine light.

With Enyo now able to defend herself, Jacob focused on decimating his own opponents. He spun around, feeling the tip of a blade cut the air in front of him. He didn't bother using a weapon—he didn't have a weapon—and instead grabbed the man's forearm and broke it with a small application of Linked Energy Manipulation. As his enemy emitted a girlish scream, Jacob crushed the pirate's ribcage with a swift punch.

Two more pirates came at him on either side. He guessed they were trying to trap him. Jacob moved back half a step, turned, and then grabbed the forearm of the pirate on his left. With a swift yank, he pulled his foe into the sword of his other enemy. The tip of a blade appeared in the pirate's back. Jacob didn't wait for them to die before kicking them into the one who'd done the stabbing.

More enemies appeared before him. They fell like wheat before a scythe. Jacob smashed into them with energy infused strength and speed. Bones broke, bodies were crushed, and people were sent flying as Jacob pounded his fists into them. He fought his way through the hordes of pirates until he and Enyo were fighting back to back.

"Why did you aim for their ship?" he asked as he plowed his fist into some poor pirate's face.

"Was I not supposed to?" asked Enyo, spinning her daggers around her hands, deflecting several swords before slitting the wrists of her two opponents. Blood gushed from the wounds like water flowing from a waterfall. "I thought that was supposed to be the signal."

"I said to shoot your magic out of the cave, not destroy their ship! Now how are we gonna get all these people home?"

"Uh… whoops?"

Out of the corner of his eye, he saw Enyo's sheepish grin. Scowling, he ducked underneath a sword, which swung over his head with a loud *whoosh!*, and then leapt up to uppercut the pirate in the jaw. Blood gushed from the man's mouth as the jaw shattered. The pirate, already dead from his neck snapping, flew through the air and hit the ground several meters away.

The scent of blood, oil, and steel filled Jacob's nose as he continued to fight. Time and again he waded through the pirates, whose numbers dwindled until there were only a dozen, and then half a dozen, and then none.

Clapping his hands as if ridding them of imaginary dust, he looked at Enyo, and then at the women who were staring at the two of them like they'd just witnessed an angel descending from heaven.

"Are those all of the captives?" he asked.

"There's one more," Enyo said. "She's somewhere else, though. Apparently, she was badmouthing the pirates and got sent to a separate cell or something."

"You go find her. I'll think up a way to get everyone out of this cave in the meantime."

"Why do I have to go find her?"

"Because you destroyed our transportation out of here."

"Ugh… it was an accident."

"And it does not change the facts. Now, go on. Make up for your destructive tendencies by rescuing that poor maiden."

"I'll show you who's a poor maiden," Enyo growled as she stalked off.

Rather than thinking up a way out of here, Jacob spent the next few moments watching Enyo walk away until she disappeared inside of the cavern.

His girlfriend had one really fine ass.

***

Jacob felt they were very fortunate. While the pirate's ship had been destroyed, they weren't the only ones living on that island. There was a tribe of people who lived on the opposite side of the island. They had come to see what all the commotion was about, apparently having felt Enyo's attack all the way on the other side of the island.

They had ships.

After bartering for passage with whatever goods were left of the pirates' haul, they and the captured women were given a ride to the Njord Peninsula. They had docked in the port town of Hargone. There, he and Enyo met with Barbosa, the town mayor, whom had been the one to originally create the quest they'd taken.

"Thank you so much for bringing those women back safely," the man blubbered as he and Enyo sat on a sofa across from him.

"You're welcome," Jacob said, trying not to show his distaste of the man's gaudy dress.

Barbossa was a man with a scary name who was about as scary as a hairless monkey wearing make up—the fact that Barbossa did, indeed, wear more makeup than most women notwithstanding. He was thin and clean shaven, and he probably would have been handsome by most women's standards.

Jacob just thought he was weird.

"It was no trouble at all," Enyo added. "We were happy to help."

"And we are very grateful for your help," Barbossa added. "Everyone's heard of the *Heroic Couple* around here. We were fortunate when you two took on this quest."

Jacob didn't want to blush, but he knew it was futile. The heat was already spreading to his cheeks.

About two months after he and Enyo started taking quests, they became known across the Njord Peninsula as the *Heroic Couple*. Apparently, several people had seen them kissing after a mission and that was how the name stuck. Enyo thought the name was cute. Jacob wanted to punch whoever had come up with it in the face.

"Now, here's your payment. Five hundred gold pieces, as promised," Barbossa said, handing the money to Jacob, who had a pouch to carry it in.

"Thank you for your business," Jacob said before he and Enyo left the man's mansion and wandered into the town.

Hargone wasn't a large town, but it was one of the largest docking towns located on the Njord Peninsula—an isolated region of Terrasole that was about ten days' travel from Alyssium. Jacob had chosen this city as their base of operations because it was, for one, so close the Alyssium that no one would expect them to live there, and two, news from Alyssium would arrive there faster than if they moved further south.

As they left, several of the women thanked him and Enyo. He took their gratitude with a smile and a nod, but he didn't otherwise focus on them. Enyo, on the other hand, basked in the attention. Jacob snorted when, as several of the women mentioned how "cool" they thought she was, Enyo puffed out her chest and grinned at everyone with a look of mixed embarrassment and arrogance.

She must have heard him, however, because she gave him the stink eye seconds later. "Something in your throat?"

"Yeah. Humor."

"Ah, that sounds like something a stick in the mud would have."

"Is that so?"

"Yes." Enyo grinned as she laced her fingers through his. "It is so."

They walked down the dirt road, and Enyo waved at several people who greeted them. Hargone consisted of many small buildings. Due to the forests up north and the natural red rock deposits inside of a mine shaft at the edge of the peninsula, the buildings were made of red bricks and wood. There was very little variation in design. The buildings were made to be sturdy in case of a hurricane.

Their destination was a bar called *The Hero's Stop*.

As they entered the room, the sound of laughter and shouts hit their ears. Their footsteps went unheard as they walked along the wooden floor. Bright lights made it easy for them to see, which made avoiding several drunken patrons easier. As they swerved around people and tables, they eventually came up to the bar, behind which a familiar woman, with hair like dusk and bright yellow eyes, stood.

"Hello, you two," Fellis said as she strolled around behind the counter. "Shall I get you the usual?"

"Yes, please," he and Enyo said at the same time.

Fellis's long black skirt swished around as she walked, and the tight black bodice that conformed to her body caused several eyes to wander lustfully. Oddly enough, she attracted more women than men, which was funny because she still claimed that it was harder for her to seduce women. As she grabbed two mugs and filled them with hot chocolate, the ruffles of her white shirt rustled.

"Here you two go." She set the mugs down in front of them. "I swear, you both drink like children."

"Alcohol is disgusting," Enyo said.

Jacob nodded. "I won't drink alcohol unless there's no other option."

"Ha..." Fellis just shook her head, as if listening to them talk exhausted her. "Whatever. Enjoy your hot chocolate."

"Ha!" One of the bar's patrons barked. "Those two make the perfect Heroic Couple! They even act like a pair of goodie two-shoes when they drink!"

"I'll shove these shoes up your ass!" Jacob shouted, which caused everyone to have a laugh at their expense.

Sadly, before anymore festivities could begin, the doors to the bar burst open like a battering ram had slammed into it. Everyone stopped talking. Heads turned. Jacob and Enyo both looked at the doorway, where they were shocked to find a familiar figure standing.

"Kindness!" Enyo shouted.

She hadn't changed much in the last few months since they had seen her. Skin the color of dusk glistened with a light sweat. Her outfit, a top that showed off her stomach, cleavage, and bare arms, attracted more than a little attention. Shapely hips were currently shaking from what must have been exhaustion, causing the flared-out pants to rustle. She was staring at Enyo and Jacob with eyes glazed over in pain.

"Finally..." she mumbled. "I finally..."

She never finished her sentence. Her eyes rolled up into the back of her head and she fell to the floor. There was an arrow sticking out of her back.

"Not good! Fellis!" Jacob called out.

Fellis already knew what he wanted. As he and Enyo rushed over to Kindness, Fellis began closing up shop. She placated the patrons as she kindly told them to leave, putting up with their wisecracks, and pinching the asses of several errant young woman who tried to cop a feel.

The men who tried to do the same she decked in the face.

Jacob knelt by Kindness, examining the arrow without pulling it out. He recognized the type. The notches in the feather gave it away. It wasn't an arrow from Terrasole. It was a Dark Clan arrow.

"Enyo, can I have one of your daggers please?" he asked softly. Enyo didn't hesitate to unsheathe one and give it to him. "Thank you."

Dark Clan arrows were unique in that they were not just designed to impale a target, but also to inflict as much pain as possible. The tips were jagged and had hooks on either end. Not only were they painful going in, they were a bitch to pull out.

Jacob knew this from having pulled several out of himself.

"If you can numb the area around her wound, that would be great," he said to Enyo, who nodded and placed her hands near the wound.

"Torpens. Privo."

White light emitted from Enyo's palms and engulfed the skin around the wound. Jacob cut away the cloth that kept him from seeing the full extent of the damage, but when he did, Enyo turned green.

"Keep it together," he murmured, not that he blamed her.

Crimson ichor poured from the wound like a flowing fountain, drenching most of Kindness's clothing. There was a gash at least six centimeters long with frayed edges as if something had torn apart her back. The arrow, impaled deeply into the wound, ripped at her muscles as she breathed.

Jacob didn't hesitate. He didn't have time to hesitate. He dug Enyo's dagger into Kindness's back, widening the hole so he could pry the arrow free without doing even more damage. His hands became slick with blood. His grip on the dagger loosened. Sweat poured down his forehead as he narrowed his eyes in concentration, keeping his focus on removing the arrow quickly without doing more harm than help.

Finally, with one last spray of blood, Jacob pried the arrow free. "Enyo!"

"Medico. Medicor. Percuro. Sicco. Emaculo."

Jacob stood up as Enyo healed Kindness's wound. He wandered behind the counter, toward the washing bowl, where he cleaned off his hands and Enyo's dagger. Fellis, who'd finished closing up shop, wandered back in and looked at Enyo.

"How is she?"

"I don't know yet." Enyo shook her head. "Her wound is horrendous. While I can heal it, she's already lost a lot of blood. I don't know if she'll survive."

"Do everything you can for her," Jacob instructed. "Fellis, prepare Kindness a bed. We should move her to somewhere more comfortable once Enyo heals her."

Fellis nodded, though she didn't leave at first. "That arrow. Jacob, do you think…?"

"We can't say anything yet," Jacob said. "However, I'm going to scout the surrounding area."

Kindness must have already been close to Hargone when she'd been shot. She wouldn't have lived long enough to reach this port town otherwise. If she had been close when receiving that wound, then it stood to reason that whoever had given it to her was still in the area.

Jacob traveled up the stairs, entered his bedroom, and grabbed the broadsword sword hanging from the wall. It felt awkward in his hand. This weapon wasn't Durandal, his partner and the only sword he'd used since he found it several years ago. It was just a regular broadsword. Decent balance. Well-made. Sharp.

It still felt off.

Traveling downstairs, Jacob offered a quick nod to Enyo and Fellis before he was out the door. He didn't stop to greet anyone, though a few of the regulars tried to ask him about Kindness, but he had no time to answer. If there really was a scouting party of Dark Clansmen out there, then he would need to find and dispose of them before they reached Hargone.

Being situated on a peninsula, Hargone was surrounded by water on three sides. The other side was all greenery. Thick palm trees grew to be six times taller than the average human. Shrubs and bushes covered most of the ground. As he ran past the trees, grass crunched underneath Jacob's feet.

There were several ledges and small cliffs in this area. They jutted up from the ground like thick, fat pillars. Jacob used those for cover and to observe his surroundings without fear of being shot. If there was a Dark Clan scouting party in the area, at least one of them would be using these ledges to provide cover fire.

As he was peering around one of the pillars, a shrill whistle cut through the air. Jacob jerked his head back. An arrow impaled the rock, sending fragments everywhere. Following the arrow to its trajectory, he found a man with pale skin and burgundy hair notching back another arrow.

Jacob didn't waste time. He channeled energy into his blade and slashed. A massive crescent shot from his sword, sailed through the air, and split apart both the stone that the Dark Clansman stood upon, and the Dark Clansman himself.

There was some shouting down below, out of his sight. The Dark Clansman's squad must have been waiting for a signal to attack. Now that their spotter was gone, they were probably going to rampage toward him.

That was fine. That was what he wanted.

Jacob channeled more energy into his blade, and then moved forward in a quick sprint. He rushed past several trees. Up ahead, five dark clansmen darted toward him. All of them were tall and skinny, with pale skin and strangely colored hair. Three of them were women, while the other two were men.

"Slice him up!" one of them shouted. The others hollered out war cries as they charged him.

Ducking under the swing of the first clansmen to attack him, Jacob ignored this person and attacked the second. His energy infused sword split their weapon in half, carving a bloody furrow from her left hip to her right shoulder. The woman he'd attacked gurgled as blood sprayed from her chest and she fell onto her back.

He didn't watch her dying spasms. An enraged cry to his left made him spin around. He raised his sword to knock aside an attack that would have impaled his stomach. He heard movement behind him. Twisting his wrist, he threw his enemy's weapon wide, stepped forward, grabbed them by the scruff of their shirt, and threw him into the person trying to sneak up behind him. As they both went down, Jacob unleashed a crescent attack that cut through them both.

"Malak! Fritza!" one of the men shouted before setting a glare on him. "Damn you!"

With a roar, the only remaining man and woman attacked him in tandem. Sadly, Dark Clansmen were not known for their teamwork. Most worked alone, the reason being their bloodlust, which made them normally impossible to work with.

Jacob had an easy time dodging their attacks. He moved left. Then right. Then he spun and kicked the scimitars out of the first one's grip. A current of air caressed his back. Jacob sidestepped. The female clansmen rushed through the space he'd been standing, her blade swinging. Before she had the chance to turn around, he sliced through her spinal cord. She fell face first to the ground and didn't get up.

The other clansmen seemed so shocked by the death of his last comrade that he never saw his death coming. His severed head rolled across the ground as his body fell, first to its knees, and then onto its chest. It twitched several times before all movement ceased.

In the quietness that accompanied his battle, Jacob could only stare at the sky and lament. He knew this day would come. He'd hoped it wouldn't, but it looked like it was true when people said that most hopes were always in vein.

Trouble had finally found them.

***

The bar was quiet when Jacob returned; the first floor was empty, and not a single noise could be heard outside of his boots scuffing against the floor.

Traveling up the stairs and walking down the hall, he came upon the guest room. While this bar was not an inn, they would allow

people who'd passed out to stay the night. It didn't happen often—
Fellis was not kind to people who couldn't walk under their own two
feet while drunk—but when it did happen, Enyo would take care of
them.

Jacob quietly opened the door, walked in, and closed it behind
him. Enyo was sitting on a chair in front of the bed. Kindness's
supine form lay upon the bed. Her shirt and shoes had been removed,
and she was lying on her back. A blanket kept her modesty intact.

"How is she?" he asked.

"She's out of danger for now," Enyo said as Jacob walked over
and stood behind her. She leaned back when he placed his hands on
her shoulders. "The wound has healed completely, and it doesn't
look like she'll be dying of blood loss. Still, it was a really close
call."

"She was lucky we were able to treat it in time."

"Yeah..."

Dark Clan arrows were deadly due to their make and shape.
Unless extracted within an hour of being shot, a person was likely to
bleed out. Jacob was honestly amazed that Kindness had been able to
make it so far. He guessed she might have been using Conjure to
stem the flow of blood.

"Come on." Jacob grabbed Enyo's hand and pulled her to her
feet. "Kindness will be fine now that she's out of danger. You need
to get some rest. You look tired."

"I feel tired," Enyo admitted.

She walked unsteadily forward before her knees buckled. Jacob
caught her before she could fall, cradling her in his arms.

"You've been sitting for so long that your legs fell asleep."

"Couldn't help it," Enyo mumbled as she placed her head
against his chest. "Until just a little while ago, I was healing
Kindness."

If she'd been healing Kindness for that long, then the woman's
wounds must have been graver than he'd expected. It had been two
hours since he'd left and gone to dispatch the scouting party. Enyo
had been working on healing her that entire time? No wonder she
seemed so weak right now. She had to have used a lot of magic.

"In that case..."

Enyo didn't resist as Jacob scooped her into his arms. She nuzzled her nose into the crook of his neck and relaxed.

"Don't fall asleep on me," he joked.

She bit his neck. "I won't."

"You say that, but you're clearly on the verge of falling asleep."

"Hmph."

Jacob walked back to his and Enyo's bedroom, entering the door and closing it with his foot. His boots made light thumps along the thick rug, which was made from a mastodon—a monstrous creature that was larger than most houses—that he and Enyo had killed one month ago. Placing Enyo on their king-sized bed, he began the laborious process of taking her clothes off.

"Come on," he said to the woman. "You can't expect me to do all this by myself."

"I expect you to do it with your teeth."

He twitched. "You want me to bite your clothes off?"

"Yes."

Enyo was speaking nonsense. This always happened when she used too much magic—when anyone used too much magic. It was a well-known physical condition called Magical Fatigue.

Magic was mental energy, the energy of the mind, and it allowed those who wielded it to change fundamental aspects of a certain nature. Darkness. Light. Metal. Elements. The ability to create something from nothing. The power to manipulate the mind. When someone used up all their magic, the mind became delirious because it didn't have the energy to function properly.

Fortunately, magic was not tied to the body, so she wouldn't die, but she would be acting loopy for a while.

"Sit up," Jacob said. Enyo did nothing. He frowned as she continued to lay there, still awake, partially cognizant, and looking at him expectantly.

This girl...

"Fine," he mumbled, taking her by the hands and pulling her until she was sitting. Even then, she slumped forward into his chest.

Getting Enyo's shirt off was a task in and of itself. Enyo was about as cooperative as sloth. She pretty much made him do all the work, and while he didn't mind pampering the girl, dealing with her when her mind was fritzing out from overusing her magic was a chore. After her shirt came her brassiere. Her breasts sprang free with a bounce, jiggling several times before coming to a stop. That done, he let her fall back onto the bed, took off her boots, socks, and then slid her off her shorts, leaving her in just her black panties.

After taking off his own clothes, Jacob lifted Enyo up once more, and then used his feet to pull the covers back. Once he set Enyo into bed, he crawled in himself and pulled up the covers. Only then did Enyo move, rolling over so she could hug him as if he was an oversized pillow.

"I notice that the only time you move during these moments is when you want something," Jacob muttered.

"I want you," Enyo mumbled, barely conscious against his chest, which she then proceeded to lick. "You taste salty."

Jacob twitched. Dealing with Enyo like this was always difficult. He was glad it rarely happened. Being the daughter of the Dark Lord Alucard, she had naturally large reserves of magic, which meant she rarely ever ran out. She'd probably run out this time because they had just finished a mission to kill several pirates, she'd gone completely overboard during said mission, healing took a lot of magic, and Kindness's wound had been extensive.

He pulled her closer and closed his eyes. "Stop licking me and go to sleep."

"You're no fun," Enyo mumbled seconds before she started snoring.

She was on the verge of passing out.

Jacob closed his eyes and fell into a light sleep.

There was no telling how much time had passed. Jacob was a light sleeper, so he was constantly aware of everything around him. Thanks to this, minutes felt like hours. The only reason sleeping was even bearable these days was because of Enyo, whose soft, warm body brought him comfort. Jacob felt like he could have stayed asleep if only to keep her with him.

Of course, because he was a light sleeper, Jacob was also aware of when Enyo woke up. She stirred against him, mumbling a little as she smacked her lips. Then she shifted. The covers peeled away as she sat up. Goosebumps broke out on his chest. Even though his eyes were still closed, he could imagine her rubbing her eyes with the back of her hand in a most adorable manner. He could feel her legs moving as she climbed on top of him.

She's going to try and surprise me...

Enyo had been trying to get the better of him for the past month. She'd wake up early and do something that he "wouldn't expect." It had become a regular occurrence, and she was always disappointed when he didn't act surprised.

I suppose I could pretend, but...

Pretending had never been his strongest points.

Thus, he opened his eyes just as Enyo was about to lean in for a kiss. She paused. Then she stared. Then she blinked several times... and then, finally, she pouted.

"When did you wake up?" she asked.

"The moment you started moving around."

The pout on her face grew larger. "That's not fair."

"Life rarely is," Jacob said with a sage-like nod.

"Don't try to sound smart," Enyo mumbled, her shoulders slumping.

Jacob withheld a chuckle as he reached behind her head and pulled Enyo into a kiss. He heard her mutter another brief "not fair" before kissing him back. Her hands went into his hair, running through his dirty blond locks. He placed his hands on the nakedness of her waist, enjoying the warmth of her soft skin.

The kiss escalated when Enyo slipped her tongue past his lips. He opened his mouth, groaning as her tongue caressed his. He moved his hands away from her waist, grabbing a handful of her ass. The lyrical gasps his actions produced was like an aphrodisiac. He loved the sound of her voice. It spurred him on further. He wanted more.

Enyo rubbed herself against him as her kiss intensified, and the feeling of her body grinding against him made Jacob's desire for her become all the stronger. He could feel himself getting sucked into her lips. It was only now, as he felt the fabric in their way, that he damned himself for not having the foresight to remove her underwear last night.

The kiss was no longer enough. Jacob pulled away. Enyo whined, but it was short-lived, as he sat up and placed his mouth on

her neck. He kissed his way up her neck, traveled along the gentle curve of her jaw, until he reached her ear.

Members of the Dark Clan had sensitive ears. During his travels, there were occasions when, to get an advantage over his enemies, Jacob would tear their ears off. It was one of the most painful things a Dark Clansmen could experience. Consequently, licking and nibbling and suckling on their ears had the opposite effect.

Enyo's cries of ecstasy resounded throughout the room, and probably across the hall. No doubt, they'd woken up Fellis if she wasn't already awake. The muscles in her butt clenched. Her body shook. Jacob could feel her lips becoming damp as her movements became more rushed. The wetness of her panties caused him to get sucked further between them. His own breathing had grown heavy as the friction caused by their ceaseless grinding sent pleasurable jolts through him.

"J-Jacob!" Enyo gasped as he bit down on her collar bone. Her arms closed around his head, preventing him from leaving.

Jacob rolled over until he was on top of her, his weight pressing against her as Enyo locked her legs around his waist. He ground his pelvis into her panties, completely damp with arousal. She cried out as her body twitched and spasmed.

He was close. They were both close. Just a little more. Just a little longer and—

"I really hate to interrupt you two when it looks like you are about to have the most mind-blowing orgasm ever," Fellis said as she opened the door. "But could you please keep it down? Our guest is embarrassed by the noise you two are making."

It felt a lot like someone had dumped a bucket full of ice water on him. Jacob's body went from blazing hot to freezing cold in seconds. He looked at Fellis, whose amused smile told him that she knew what she was doing—the cock blocker. He then looked at Enyo. The glare she sent Fellis could have cut through a mountain.

"I hate you so much right now," Enyo said.

Fellis just smiled. "But I love you. Now, you two should get dressed... actually, wash off first, and then get dressed. Kindness has something important to tell you, but I don't think it would be appropriate to talk to her while smelling like sex."

Gritting her teeth, Enyo, in a bitter voice, said, "We didn't have sex, no thanks to you."

"I live to please," Fellis said before disappearing.

Jacob listened as her footsteps and laughter receded, and then he sighed. "I guess we'd better get ready."

"Yeah," Enyo grumbled as she climbed off him. "Damn that Fellis."

While neither of them were pleased by Fellis's interruption, they did follow her instructions and washed off. While their inn had a bath, they didn't use it, since it took time to prepare the water. Instead, they just rinsed each other off wash rags and soap from a basin of water, and then dressed once they were dry.

Kindness was already awake when they entered the bedroom. She looked at them—and then blushed and promptly looked away. Yes, Jacob realized, she had definitely heard them. Maybe their activities were what woke her up in the first place.

That... was kind of embarrassing, actually.

"I'm glad you're awake," Enyo said as she sat down. Her cheeks were red, but she admirably withheld her own mortification. "How are you feeling?"

"I-I'm, um, good," Kindness muttered, eyeing her and Jacob like she'd never met them before. "I feel... much better. You healed me, right? Thank you."

Enyo shook her head. "Don't worry about that. You're a friend... though I'm really surprised to see you. I didn't expect us to meet again."

At those words, Kindness seemed to finally get over her embarrassment. Her expression turned grave. "I normally would not have come, since I know what would happen if the kingdom learned of your location, but I... something has happened that mandated my coming."

"It has something to do with the Dark Clan," Jacob said as he stood by the end of the bed. "They've invaded Terrasole, haven't they?"

"It's more complicated than that," Kindness said. "About two months ago, both Justice and Abstinence were killed. We found them in their mansions with their throats slit. A little while after that, Chastity disappeared, and then about a month later, a large army of Dark Clansmen and monsters appeared on our doorstep."

Jacob blew out a deep breath. Enyo, meanwhile, looked like she'd been sucker punched.

"That... that is unexpected."

"It gets worse," Kindness said. "None of our scouts have been able to figure out what's happening in the surrounding lands north of Alyssium. We don't know if the cities and villages are even still there. What's more, Alyssium has been under siege ever since then. Our people are dying, our army is powerless, and Queen Alice and myself aren't enough to protect them."

"And that's why you're here," Enyo realized. "You came to ask for our help."

Kindness bowed her head. "I know that you have no reason to help us. I understand that we have wronged you greatly. However, for the sake of my people, I have come to swallow my pride and ask for your help. Enyo. Jacob. Will you two please save our kingdom?"

Enyo looked at Jacob, her eyes asking a silent question. She was leaving this decision to him. Because he was the one who'd been hurt the most by Alyssium, she was letting him make the decision, even though he could see the desire to help clear as day in her eyes.

He ran a hand through his hair. This decision had already been taken out of his hands.

"We'll help," he said.

Kindness looked at him with wide, hope-filled eyes. "You will?"

"Yes, we will." Jacob held up two fingers. "On two conditions."

Kindness bit her lip. "I... cannot promise anything, but name those conditions, and I'll do everything in my power to see them met."

As Jacob stated the terms for their help, Kindness's eyes widened. He didn't know if she would be able to help. He didn't know if Queen Alice would even agree to these conditions. However, in this moment, Jacob took a chance.

It was likely the only one he would ever get.

INTERLUDE IV - RED TIDINGS

Alice stared out the window of Avant Heim. The war had taken its toll on both her and her kingdom. The once pristine buildings now lay in ruins; there were many gutted out buildings that barely stood and some that were demolished entirely. Large boulders lay scattered, remnants of the catapults that had destroyed the buildings. The walls surrounding Alyssium were, thankfully, still intact, but it would only be a matter of time before even that was breached.

Her soldiers were exhausted and disheartened, her people were frightened, and the White Council, the most powerful magicians at her disposal, had been reduced to a single person—and Kindness had disappeared about three weeks ago. What's more, they were short on supplies, their hospitals were filled with injured, and they didn't have enough medicine to go around.

It would take a miracle to win.

Listy stood behind her. Silent. Strong. Without her support, Alice might have given up hope. Weighed down by everything that had happened, hurt because of the things she'd done for the good of her kingdom, and angry at herself because one of the only people who could've helped her was now gone, Alice no longer had the strength to do anything on her own.

At the time, imprisoning Jacob had seemed like the right thing to do. He'd been aiding and abetting a criminal, and even if he hadn't, his battle had destroyed a good portion of Tallus Caelum. As queen, she could not show mercy to anyone who committed a crime, not even to him. Those had been her thoughts at the time.

She'd never regretted those thoughts more than she did now.

"Do you think I did the right thing?" she asked.

Listy shifted. "I think… you did the only thing you could at the time."

"Yes, and look at where that has gotten us." She placed her gloved hand on the window. "My people are terrified, my soldiers are dying, and the White Council is no more. Even with Freya returning, we are hopelessly outmatched."

Freya, the greatest warrior of her kingdom, a former companion of Jacob during his quest to slay Alucard, had returned last week to assist her in this time of need. Alice did not know where the woman had disappeared to. Still, she'd come back, and Alice was grateful for her presence. Her skills in combat, her ability to single-handedly destroy an entire battalion of Dark Clansmen, had given her knights hope.

It still wasn't enough.

One person could not hope to turn the tide of battle, save maybe Jacob. As the slayer of the Dark Lord, he wielded incredible power, not just physically, but morally, for both enemy and ally alike. His presence would have bolstered her soldiers and frightened her enemies.

Even if he was but a single man, sometimes, the presence of a legendary figure was all anyone needed to feel emboldened.

To her words, Listy could say nothing. She might not have gotten along with Jacob because of how Alice had always been sneaking off with him when they were younger, but she couldn't deny the truth in Alice's words.

The doors opening with a low groan made Alice turn. Bayard rushed into the room, his harried face covered in sweat and his tired eyes containing bags underneath them.

"Your majesty," he said breathlessly. "The dark army has begun its siege again."

The dark army, led by a woman named Lust, had stationed their base several leagues away. Since their last battle two nights ago, there'd not been a peep from them. Alice had dared to hope that the army would retreat. It was a vain hope, she knew, but the disappointment that it had not happened remained like the bitter aftertaste of bad wine.

"Prepare my armor," Alice said with the strong and indomitable voice of a queen, commanding and stern.

"At once, your majesty," Listy said with a low bow.

Alice marched to the armory, Listy and Bayard trailing after her. In this place, hundreds of weapons and armor suits sat, unused and gathering dust. They were the armor and weapons of previous rulers. Golden suits that normally gleamed were dull, weapons sat unused in racks, and chests remained unopened and worn. Among these many weapons and armored suits, three objects were pristine.

"If it isn't Alice," Durandal said in a mocking voice. "It's been two days since I last saw you. Are you here to try and wield me again?"

"Not this time," Alice said dryly. "I've learned my lesson."

The last time she had tried to wield Durandal, the sword had shocked her hand so badly it got burned. Then it had mocked her after the fact. Listy had actually tried to throw it out, but the sword had shocked her as well. No one was able to touch it. It was a wonder they had even managed to store it in here.

"A good idea. I'm glad to see you're so quick on the uptake," Durandal said, its metallic voice mocking.

Alice ignored the sword as Listy helped put her armor on. The chest plate that she wore was silver with gold edgings, though the metal was dented from the previous battle. They'd not had time to repair it. Shoulder pauldrons went on next, followed by knee high boots with metal shinguards and scratched vambraces that had once been cast in gold. The final touch was a sword. It was attached to her waist.

"Hey, hey," Durandal continued to talk as her armor was being put on. "I've got a good joke for you: What is the similarity between a woman and a laxative? They both irritate the crap out of you!"

Durandal went ignored. This was not the first, second, or even fourteenth time that the sword had spewed vulgar and insulting jokes. Supposedly, its maker had loved dirty jokes. Alice just thought the sword was a creep.

Tightening her vambraces, Alice and Listy exited the weapons vault, leaving behind Durandal, who continued spewing insulting jokes.

Bayard was waiting for them outside. "Your Majesty, are you ready?"

"Yes," Alice said, turning to Listy. "Please tell the medics and healers to return to their stations. Remember, you'll be in charge should I perish."

"Please don't say things like that," Listy said.

Alice could only offer a smile.

With Bayard at her side, she exited the castle and took a carriage to the main gate. Freya stood before an array of troops. Caslain was beside her. Unlike the nervous young paladin, the warrior famous for her skills with a spear wore a broad and somewhat frightening grin, as though she welcomed the opportunity to slay more enemies.

"Alice, it's a good day for battle," she said.

"You think every day is a good day for battle," Alice replied, rolling her eyes.

"Aye, but I have a feeling that today will be an especially good day," Freya said with a twinkle in her eyes.

Alice rolled her eyes again, but the words did her a wonder of good. The situation was dire. They were outnumbered, outmatched, and on the brink of defeat. Yet even so, Freya could smile and joke like it was just another day. Her courage and fearlessness gave Alice strength.

At the top of the gate, where several hundred bowmen stood at the ready, Alice looked over the field, at the army that stood several kilometers away.

The dark army consisted of more than just Dark Clansmen. Trolls and ogres stood within their ranks. Goblins had taken the front, acting as fodder for her bowmen's arrows. Further behind that was an elephanté, a massive creature that was covered in armor designed for breaking down giant doors—a living battering ram.

That's new...

Searching her out, Alice found the woman who was leading this army. She sat in the center, body languidly resting on a throne. Chastity was with the woman. Through her telescope, she could see the drool leaking from his mouth and the insane gleam in his eyes. Whatever remained of the once ambitious man was gone. He'd become nothing but a puppet.

There was a moment's pause. The entire world seemed to hold its breath. Then the army before her, a massive horde of monsters and Dark Clansmen, charged forward with vicious cries and raging bellows.

Alice gave a grim smile.

This would likely be her last battle.

CHAPTER 6 - LUST FOR ENTERTAINMENT

Since they were stressed for time, Jacob bought several horses off the money he and Enyo had earned from their last quest. If all went according to plan, he wouldn't need it anyway.

Alyssium was ten days by foot and three by horse. They first had to travel through the forests of the Njord Peninsula, after which they would reach Kaolin, a city about half the size of Alyssium.

A sense of disparity hung over the city. People looked over their shoulders, mothers gripped their children's hands, and several shops and homes were boarded up. The fear emitting from the people was an almost palpable thing, a physical sensation that made his skin crawl.

"It's because of the war," Kindness had explained. "Everyone here knows that Alyssium is under attack. They know that if Alyssium falls, there will be no hope for them. The Dark Clan will wash over this community like a tidal wave. Everyone here will get swept up, either becoming slaves to their new masters or being killed off for amusement."

"Not all of us are like that, you know," Fellis said.

"Yes, you are correct." Kindness amended with a nod. "However, the ones that are under Lust's command are exactly as I described."

Fellis was forced to concede the woman's point with a nod.

They didn't stay in Kaolin for long, barely a single night, as they woke up before the sun had risen and journeyed off again. While it was important to rest, they needed to reach Alyssium quickly. According to Kindness, Alice and her knights had been in bad shape when she left. There was no telling how bad things were now.

Jacob may not have liked what Alice had done to him, but the last thing he wanted was for her and the kingdom to fall.

The area around Kaolin consisted of rolling hills and grassy plains. There were a few errant monsters, but nothing that could slow them down. After several hours of travel, they reached the forests surrounding Alyssium. Sadly, their horses didn't like the forest, wouldn't even go in no matter how much they tried to push them onward, and so they had to go around.

What they found upon taking the scenic route was a war-torn land and a city under siege. The roadside was trampled with footprints. They ranged from human-shaped prints to massive animal paws. The group traveled further, eventually reaching Alyssium.

They were already late to the party. Ladders with hooks were latched onto the walls. The massive door that kept people from going in and out at night was gone, only a broken frame and the busted remains there to show what it had once been. Beyond the wall, Jacob could see the one responsible, a giant elephanté that was rampaging through the city.

The city was engulfed in flames.

"Oh, no!" Kindness stared in horror.

"It's not over yet," Jacob said with a grim frown. "I can see people still fighting."

Enyo, sitting behind Jacob since she didn't know how to ride, shifted in order to reach for her daggers. "Then what are we waiting for? Let's get in there and help!"

No one argued. As one, they whipped on their reigns and sent their steeds into battle. They were only riding two horses, so Enyo rode on the back of his while Kindness rode on Fellis's.

Most of the enemy army was already inside of the city. The few that remained were stragglers and easily dealt with by Kindness's magic. The woman chanted as she held onto Fellis. Several spears appeared in the air, and those spears shot forward and impaled numerous enemies, who went down with squeals of pain or death gurgles.

They rushed past the gates. Enyo buried her face into his neck, though he couldn't blame her. Everywhere he looked, corpses lined the streets. Most of the dead were monsters, goblins and trolls, but there were also a few Dark Clansmen and humans. They lay with their bodies broken, their limbs twisted. Blood leaked from wounds. Pools of red spread from underneath them, while sightless eyes stared at the sky

Some of the humans were civilians.

The fighting had moved deeper into the city, and since it would no longer be safe to ride horseback, they dismounted and sent their steeds away with a swat to the rear.

Pulling out his sword, Jacob lamented once again that he did not have Durandal with him. That sword was rude, lewd, and loud, but it was the only blade that could withstand his full power. It had been specifically made for channeling chi through it.

He sighed before straightening himself out. "We're traveling to the palace! However, we can't leave these people to fend for themselves. Let's split up into two groups to cover more ground. Fellis and Enyo, you two are going together. Kindness, you're with me."

Everyone agreed. They broke off and went in separate directions. Jacob and Kindness took the left. A scream rang out somewhere up ahead. They took an alley, ran through it, and came out the other side to find two goblins attacking a young woman trying to protect her child.

"Acer. Acutus. Acidus."

A spear formed in the air and flew forward. Blood splashed against the pavement as it went through the goblin on the left. In that time, Jacob had already sent a crescent attack that cut the other goblin in half.

He went up to the mother. "Get inside of one of these buildings. Hide under a bed or in a closet and don't come out until the guards come to get you!"

Her eyes wide, the woman nodded several times, and pulled her crying son along behind her.

Jacob only stuck around long enough to make sure the woman really did head inside of a building. Then he and Kindness ran off in search of the next person to help.

"Question," Kindness said as they ran.

"Yes?"

"Why did you have me come with you and not Enyo?"

Jacob leapt over a fallen corpse. Up ahead, a troll appeared in their path, large and lumbering. He didn't bother waiting for it to notice them and sliced it in half with a crescent blade. A crack suddenly appeared on his blade.

This isn't going to last much longer...

"Because Enyo is stronger than you," Jacob said bluntly. "You're also more suited toward long range combat. Meanwhile, Fellis doesn't have a strong combat magic and can only act as support. If I had gone with Enyo, then our parties would have been uneven."

"I see..."

Jacob didn't know what she was thinking, but he honestly didn't care. A group of Dark Clansmen were up ahead. They were killing several people, innocent civilians, and he would be damned if he let them continue.

Energy raced through his body. His muscles became stronger, sturdier, faster. He shot forward, the ground indenting underneath him. Appearing before the Dark Clansmen, Jacob sliced through the first enemy before they even realized he was among them. The scent of blood stung his nostrils, but he ignored it, attacking the next enemy instead. His blade cleaved them from left hip to right shoulder.

It wasn't until the second one fell by his hands that they realized they were in trouble, but it was already too late. Kindness had chanted a spell. Six spears appeared in the air, and all of them shot forward, piercing flesh with ease. Not all of them were killing hits, but Jacob dispatched those that hadn't died.

He turned to the four civilians who were left alive. "Get inside! Find a place to hide! Don't come out until the guards come!"

Not waiting to see if they would follow his orders, he leapt onto the roof. From there, he could see more of the fighting. It looked like much of the fighting in this district was done. All of the monster forces had congregated at the castle. Even as he watched, the doors to the castle were shattered and the monsters spilled in.

"Damn it!" Looking down, Jacob shouted to Kindness. "Avant Heim has been breached! I'm going up ahead!"

"You're leaving me?!" Kindness shouted in shock.

He grimaced. He couldn't very well leave her. Powerful magician or not, she had no talent for close range combat. If she faced too many enemies, then she would fall.

Leaping down, he gave the woman no time to protest as he scooped her into his arms and leapt back onto the roof.

"What do you think you're doing?!"

"Sorry, but we're in rush! Hang on tight!"

"Hang on? What are you talking abooOOOUUUUTTTT!!!!"

Air slammed into Jacob's face as he leapt across the roof, his speed increasing by sending energy through his muscles. His eyes watered as the world around him blurred. He could actually feel his lips flapping as he moved, and screaming in his ear, Kindness drowned out everything. Despite this, he didn't stop running until they'd reached Avant Heim.

When they got there, the front gate was in shambles. Beyond that, the courtyard was covered in corpses.

"Jacob!" Enyo shouted as she rushed up from the park. Her daggers were out and covered in blood. Behind her, Fellis was favoring her left leg.

"Let's get in there quickly! We need to make sure Alice and the others are okay!" Jacob said.

Rushing up the stairs, Jacob ran past several corpses and into the hallway. The sound of blades clashing echoed all around them. Oil and steel tinged with blood invaded their noses.

"We should split up again," Fellis suggested.

"Agreed," Kindness said. "We need to find Queen Alice."

"Let's all separate," Enyo said. "We'll be able to cover ground more quickly, and if one of us finds Alice, we can alert the others by causing a lot of noise… or something."

Everyone stared at her, eventually forcing Enyo to look away.

"It was just a suggestion," she muttered.

"There's no need to split up. You three should head to the Great Hall. If Alice isn't dead, then she'll be making her last stand there," Jacob told them.

"How do you know that?" asked Fellis. When Jacob gave her a flat stare, she looked away. "Right. Stupid question."

"It was. Now get going."

"What about you?" asked Enyo.

"I can't fight all out unless my partner is with me."

He, of course, meant Durandal. As a sentient blade forged from an unknown metal, it was the only sword that could withstand his power. His other weapon had already cracked. One more burst of energy and it would break.

They split up, Enyo and her group traveling toward the Great Hall, while he went toward the one place his weapon would be.

If Durandal was anywhere, it would be in the weapons vault, which was locked, of course, and by a big steel door no less. The door didn't stop him. Jacob kicked it with energy enhanced strength. While a jolt traveled up his leg, the door dented and opened. He walked in.

"Partner!"

Durandal was inside. Jacob strolled up, grabbed the blade, and strapped it across his shoulder.

"Sorry, but we don't have time to deal with a touching reunion right now. Alyssium is under siege."

"Hmph! Good riddance, I say. Damn broads couldn't take a single joke."

"Considering your brand of humor, I don't blame them."

"How mean!" Durandal cried. "How nostalgic!"

"Easy, you masochistic sword."

Knowing that time was of the essence, Jacob bolted out of the weapons vault and traveled toward the Great Hall. He hoped Enyo and the others were okay.

***

Enyo was a whirlwind. With nothing but a horde of enemies in front of her, she took no issue with letting her dark blood run wild. It pulsed within her, a ferocious beat that demanded to be satiated with blood, and she heeded its call.

"Obscurim. Opscurum. Obscuritas." Enyo channeled as the dark blood within flooded her nerves. "Exidio. Excisio. Exscidium."

Darkness appeared before her, a never-ending wave that washed through the hall, a ceaseless flame that shrieked as if made from tormented spirits. The black fire engulfed everything, everyone. It burned all in its path. When it vanished, there was nothing left. Everything had been turned to ash.

Kindness gulped. "I did not know you were also a dark magic user."

"Few people know that," Fellis said.

They continued moving. Enyo led from the front. She took enemies out with her magic, and when that didn't work, her daggers did the trick. Blood spurted from wounds. The floor and walls were painted crimson. Enyo could see nothing except what was in front of her. It felt like she was rushing through a tunnel. Everything else was invisible as she ran, ducked, dodged, wove, and killed.

Several knights appeared in front of her. Had this been several months ago, they would have died too, a result of her inability to control the dark pulse in her veins. Thanks to Jacob, she could accept this side of her. His support had given her the strength to accept her other half, the Dark Clan half that enjoyed battle and bloodshed. Thanks to him, she could now control who she directed that bloodlust at.

The knights barely had time to notice her as she rushed by them. She brushed them without harming a single knight, instead slitting the throats of the enemies they were fighting, freeing them up and allowing them to fight more enemies.

The Great Hall was a mess by the time they arrived. Pillars had crumbled to dust. Broken bodies clad in armor lay strewn about, their limbs twisted, their faces etched into one's of horror.

At the opposite side, standing before a dais, Alice, Listy, and a woman who Enyo didn't know fought against a horde of Dark Clansmen. The woman she didn't know was like a dancer. She twirled the staff around in her hands. Every time she attacked, a large blade like Jacob's crescent attack shot out, and Dark Clan members were slaughtered by the handful.

Lust stood behind the horde, laughing as she watched Alice, Listy, and the female knight struggle. Standing beside her, Chastity stared at everything with eyes that gleamed of insanity.

"That's it! Yes! Keep fighting! Don't stop! I want to see the despair in your eyes when you finally realize how futile your continued struggle is!"

"Damn bitch likes to talk a lot," the female knight said, her voice strained. Enyo didn't need to know her to figure out that she was close to breaking.

"Nox. Umbra. Dissulto."

A tug at her navel preluded her attack. A dark sphere of energy soared at Lust, though it was quickly intercepted by a golden shield that sprang up in front of her.

"Oh, dear. It seems we have uninvited guests," Lust muttered. "And if it isn't the Dark Lady. My apologies, Dark Lady, but I don't have time to deal with you right now. Why don't you run along? I'll capture you eventually… when I'm done here."

"I don't think so! Nox. Umbra. Moltus."

Hundreds of tiny black spheres appeared in the air, hovering for but a moment before they shot forward at a rapid rate.

Lust laughed as another shield sprang up around her. The spheres bounced off harmlessly. However, she wasn't their real target.

Chastity, despite his mind being gone, had enough sense to dodge, or perhaps it was because he'd been left with nothing but instincts that he could dodge. He avoided all the spheres, his movements oddly boneless. He reminded Enyo of a snake.

"Penetro. Percutio. Truso."

A large spear coalesced into existence. Its blade, shaped like a leaf, had a foreign appearance. It was unremarkable aside from that, but it shot forward with unerring accuracy. Chastity couldn't fully dodge, distracted as he was, and he howled when the blade impaled his left shoulder.

"Enyo, leave this man to me," Kindness said. "I dislike violence, but I owe this man for all the pain and death he's caused."

"I understand," Enyo accepted these terms. "Fellis!"

"I'm here! Let's get Lust!"

Lust's beatific smile overflowed with condescension as Enyo and Fellis moved on either side of her. Her posture bespoke of nothing but the utmost confidence.

"Two on one? That hardly seems like a fair fight," she taunted.

"A Dark Council member with hundreds of years of experience against an eighteen-year-old and someone barely in her thirties is perfectly fair," Enyo fired back. "Fuvis. Nubilus. Displodo."

The ground underneath Lust erupted with black energy. It was avoided when their foe leapt into the air. Enyo timed her next attack. Her goal was to hit Lust as she was descending.

She didn't descend. She remained in the air, floating.

"Nice try," Lust laughed. "Now, let's see you two dodge this!"

Enyo felt panic as several dozen balls of fire descended like falling stars. She leapt across the floor. Heat washed over her as the balls struck the ground, detonating with enough force to throw her backwards.

She skidded along the ground, her hands moving up to cover her face. Marble shards pelted her body, battering her, stabbing her. She felt blood leak from cuts. Fire flared along her flesh.

A little ways over, Fellis wasn't doing much better, and in fact, she might have been doing worse. Her teeth were grit and sweat ran down her face. Back. Forth. Left. Right. She was a never-ending stream of movement, but she also wasn't as fast as Enyo. Several fireballs came dangerously close to scorching her.

Enyo gnashed her teeth together. She wasn't going to let herself be toyed with. Channeling magic into her daggers, she swung at the next fireball to descend on her, splitting it in half. The crescent continued forward, forcing Lust to move out of the way.

There was a frown on her face. "I see you've learned to adapt the hero's technique to your own repertoire. Tell me, Dark Lady, are you bedding him?"

"So what if I am?"

"Ho?" Lust chuckled. "I have no problem with it, though the Dark Council will be quite displeased to learn that you've been despoiled. You know that ruins all their plans to create a new Dark Lord, yes?"

"Like I care," Enyo said dryly as she launched another crescent at Lust. It was dodged again. "Are you going to stay up there all day? You'll run out of magic before I'm even half empty."

Lust scoffed. "You underestimate my powers, girl. Still, I suppose you have a point. It wouldn't be much fun if I killed you from up here."

Without warning, Lust suddenly swooped down. Enyo barely had time to move before the woman was upon her.

A sword of darkness had appeared in her hand, and she swung it with enough power that Enyo was knocked backwards when she tried to block.

Her hands stung from blocking the strike. She almost dropped her daggers, though it was a good thing she clenched them tightly, because Lust came in swinging again.

I can't let those hit me!

Enyo backpedaled to gain distance. Lust followed. The dagger in her left hand went flying when Lust struck again. With only one hand left to block, she had no choice but to dodge. However, dodging proved more difficult than she imagined.

She ducked. Several strands of hair were cut from her head. Before she could stand up, a knee appeared in her face. Shock raced through Enyo as she fell backwards, rolled along the ground, and jumped back onto her feet.

Six spears made of water were all that greeted her. They flew in. She ducked. Fire raced through her veins as blood appeared on her arms and legs when she couldn't quite dodge several of them.

Lust laughed at her, grinning as if her suffering was a vintage wine meant to be savored. She charged at Enyo—tried to charge. A whip had wrapped around her waist.

"Don't forget about me," Fellis said with a feral grin. "Now, Enyo!"

"Nox. Praemium."

A ball of condensed energy appeared and shot toward Lust, but it slammed against a slab of marble that sprung from the ground when Lust stamped her left foot. The marble exploded, sending shards flying everywhere. Lust mumbled something under her breath, and suddenly, the shards all reoriented themselves and shot at Fellis, who's surprised scream echoed around the Great Hall.

"Fellis!" Enyo shouted, yet the moment she tried to help her friend, she was the one being attacked.

"Oh, no!" Lust cackled as her condensed blade of dark matter slammed into Enyo's remaining dagger. Enyo's knees buckled. "You're not going anywhere. The fun is just beginning!"

Enyo tried to dodge the incoming sword swing instead of blocking. She was met with several fireballs for her trouble. Screaming as the tiny spheres of flame burnt her skin, she moved back, which brought her directly in line with Lust and her madly swinging blade again. The dagger in her hand was knocked out. Then she was kicked in the gut. She doubled over as all the oxygen was expelled from her lungs, and then flew backwards when the force of Lust's kick launched her into the air.

Her world exploded as she slammed back first into the ground, tumbled across the floor, and stopped several meters away. She blinked several times. It was a vain attempt to get the spots from her eyes. She tried to suck in a breath, but it wouldn't come. All she could do was gasp in pained asphyxia.

A shadow appeared over her. Lust stared down at her. She seemed... disappointed.

"Is this really all you have to offer?" Lust asked, the dark sword wavering in her hand. "How disheartening."

She raised the sword and brought it down. Enyo could only watch as it fell.

A figure appeared in front of her. Blood splashed against her face. Enyo's eyes were wide as she screamed.

"FELLIS!"

***

It took Jacob less than five minutes to reach the Great Hall. When arrived, the room was in chaos. Pillars had been shattered, bodies were burning with black fire, walls had been demolished. In the center of this chaos was Enyo, whose enraged screams were accompanied by waves of black energy that washed over everything with frightening indiscrimination.

Kindness stood by the dais, protecting Alice, Listy and a shockingly familiar face. She had conjured a barrier out of a glowing substance that reminded him of molten metal. The shield did its job, protecting them from the flames and dark energy that Enyo was tossing around like confetti at a parade.

Jacob snuck over to Kindness and the others. He had to circumvent the room, and by the time he reached them, the roof had been destroyed.

"Kindness," he said. "What's going on? Why is Enyo going on a rampage?"

"J-Jacob!" Alice gasped as she saw him. He couldn't pay her much attention. He could only nod in acknowledgement.

"It's... Fellis... she's dead." Jacob wondered if the stab to his heart was a physical pain. It certainly felt like someone had impaled him with a sword. "She died protecting Enyo."

Jacob had experienced the death of comrades before. When he journeyed to defeat the Dark Lord, there were plenty of people who had died in his company. It always hurt. Perhaps due to how they'd been living together for the past four months, learning that Fellis was dead hurt more than any one death he'd witnessed.

"I can understand why she's rampaging now," Jacob said before hardening his resolve. "But we can't let her continue. If she keeps this up, then our goal of saving this kingdom will go up in flames."

"You want to save Terrasole?" Alice asked, flabbergasted.

"I mostly just wanted to save you," Jacob admitted. "However, Terrasole is as much a part of you as your own limbs. Besides, I may have given up on being a hero, but that doesn't mean I'm willing to let innocent people die right in front of me."

"You've grown up," Freya said. "I wonder where that little know-it-all brat went?"

"He died in the darklands," Jacob said. "By the way, what are you doing here? Weren't you going on a journey?"

"Is now the time for such questions?"

"I guess not."

Beyond the barrier, which Jacob was reinforcing with his energy, Enyo was still locked in a vicious struggle against Lust. But even with her bloodlust and hatred fueling her, she was losing. Lust remained calm as she dispersed all of Enyo's attacks, laughing as she did so.

"If you three could keep Lust occupied, I'll bring Enyo to her senses," Jacob said.

"I take it you have a plan?" Alice asked.

"Of course he doesn't have a plan," Durandal said.

Jacob smacked the sword's hilt to make it be quiet. "Just leave it to me. Kindness?"

"Coangusto. Ligo. Relligo. Alligo," Kindness chanted.

A rope composed of what looked like liquid metal appeared around Lust. The woman barely had time to blink before the binding was constricting around her, pinning her arms to her side. They didn't last long. She burned through them in a split second, but that was enough time for Enyo to leave a painful gash on her side.

Jacob burst from behind the barrier. Alice, Kindness, and Freya followed, while Listy stayed behind. Their targets were different, however. Jacob was heading straight for Enyo, whose enraged howling was sounding less human by the second. The other three went for Lust, attacking her in concert.

"Have you three finally decided to crawl out of your hole and die?" Lust asked.

"The only one dying today is you!" Alice shouted as she swung her sword at the woman. It was avoided with ease. Lust laughed as she swung her own blade, the dark matter composing it crackling. Alice was able to dodge thanks to her magic: Foresight.

Before Lust could attack Alice again, Freya leapt in and swung her spear, unleashing a crescent of energy. While Lust dodged by leaping away, her move took her right in the path of several arrows that Kindness had conjured. This forced her to bring up a shield, which Freya broke through by thrusting her spear forward.

As that was going on, Jacob tackled Enyo to the ground. The girl released a surprised squawk. Her eyes, hazed over with red, didn't even seem to see him. She struggled underneath him, trying to spear him through the chest, but he grabbed her hand before it could pierce him. Then he shoved her hand away...

... and slapped her.

"Wake up, Enyo!" Jacob shouted. "Do you think Fellis would be happy that you're acting like an animal? You need to get ahold of yourself!"

Enyo blinked several times, as if just now realizing who he was. "Jacob?"

"It's me."

"Jacob..." Tears formed in her eyes. "Jacob, Fellis is... Fellis is..."

Explosions followed by howling laughter and loud chants rang out behind them. Jacob felt heat wash over his back from intense flames. He heard the ground shattering like refuse being pulverized by the fist of an angry god.

Jacob's tongue felt thick as he said, "I know it hurts, but you can't let her death ruin you. She wouldn't want you to act like this. If you do this, if you lash out and rampage like this, her sacrifice will be in vain."

"But it hurts..."

"I know." Jacob narrowed his eyes. "And that's why we're gonna get revenge, but not like this. Come on, Enyo. Get up and help me put this bitch down. For Fellis."

Enyo sniffled back the tears in her eyes. She nodded. "Okay."

Jacob stood up, pulling Enyo to her feet. Several meters away, the battle between Lust and the others was not going well. Despite it being three on one, Lust avoided or blocked every attack sent her way.

Alice's sword was knocked aside when she tried to attack, and then her armor was dented as a large root split the ground and smacked her away. Her scream was silenced when she slammed into a wall.

Freya swung her blade and twirled around Lust with a dancer's grace, but her every move was predicted and countered. Before the woman could continue, several more roots sprouted from the ground, entangling her legs. Lust then sent a vile wave of dark energy. It was split in half, but that was only a distraction. The real attack came in the form of a knife, which would have impaled Freya's left eye if she didn't have such excellent reflexes. Yet even though she knocked it back, she was still forced to retreat.

Chanting under her breath, Kindness created numerous spears that shot at Lust. None of them reached the woman. She chanted something as well and a large dome of fire appeared around her. The spears evaporated as if they were water. Kindness and Freya were then launched across the great hall when an incredible, invisible force slammed into them.

"Oh? I see you two are finally ready to begin our final showdown?" Lust licked her lips. "You don't know how long I've been waiting for this, hero. Ever since our battle in Tallus Caelum, I haven't been able to get you out of my mind."

"I'm not sure if I should be flattered or disgusted," Jacob said.

"I'd be flattered," Durandal added.

"Shut up, D."

Lust shuddered as a warm blush lit her pale cheeks and her breathing grew heavy. "You don't know how long I've been waiting to feel these emotions again, to feel alive again. Come, you two." Her lips splitting into a grin that showed off her pearly whites, Lust gestured for them. "Come and make me feel alive!"

Jacob rushed forward, Durandal singing as he swung the blade faster than the human eye could blink. It was blocked by Lust. However, the force of his swing was powerful enough that she was lifted off her feet and sent sailing through the air. Jacob didn't hesitate. He leapt after her.

Appearing above her in a burst of speed, Jacob swung Durandal again. Lust cackled as she, once more, blocked his attack. Since she was flying horizontally to the ground, she was slammed against the floor, which cratered underneath her.

Jacob didn't have anything stopping him. He continued soaring through the air. He flipped around, landing on his feet and skidding across the floor. In that time, Enyo had finished chanting a rather long incantation.

A large wall of dark matter appeared above the crater. Tendrils of energy like arcs of lightning skittered across its crackling surface. On her command, the wall fell, slamming into the ground, crushing the floor, and then exploding with a terrific howl that reminded Jacob of damned souls screaming in agony.

Did that kill her?

It didn't. Laughter erupted from within the explosion of energy, which dispersed seconds later as a powerful gust of wind and energy burst from the center. Lust, her clothing torn and blood running down her head, wore the largest grin that he'd ever seen. It was a joyful grin, a spirited grin, the kind a child might give when they were having fun.

"Yes! Yes, that's it! This is the feeling that I've longed for! More! Give me more!"

Lust raised her hands into the air as though preparing to conduct an orchestra. Roots erupted from the ground, large and thick, twisted and gnarled, they plowed through the floor, ascending higher and higher before they broke through the roof. Then they came back down to crush him and Enyo.

Jacob didn't think. He just acted.

His body enhanced, he moved across the floor, weaving between roots as he grabbed Alice, Freya, and Kindness. The wall before them was gone, demolished during Enyo's fight with Lust before he had arrived. Jacob threw all three of them outside.

He turned around. Enyo was trapped by several roots. He could see occasional flashes of her as she launched blades of dark energy, slicing roots apart with every swing. Up above them, standing on one of the roots, Lust laughed down at them both.

"That's right! Fight! Struggle! Let me see your determination burning brighter than ever before I snuff it out!"

She talks a lot. Has she gone insane?

Jacob launched himself into the air, high above Lust, and then descended right toward her. Durandal sung as it sliced the air. His attack, which would have cut the woman in two, was blocked by a hand. The root underneath her cracked, but she did not budge.

"Why, hello there," Lust said with a smile—right before she smashed a glowing ball of energy into his face.

Jacob yelped as the light blinded him and burned his skin. He felt the air in front of him shift and leapt back. A cool breeze struck his skin. His shirt had been torn.

Rubbing his eyes, Jacob landed on the ground and blinked several times. Sixteen roots the size of the columns that once stood in this hall met his returned vision.

"Partner!"

"I know!"

Jacob slid his feet apart and swung Durandal. Twenty-six cuts were made in less than a second. A blade of energy erupted each time he attacked. The roots were sliced apart. Sadly, just as he assumed the danger from them had passed, those sliced up chunks ignited and flew at him.

"HA!"

Swinging Durandal down, Jacob generated an incredible gust of wind. What remained of the marble floor was ripped apart, the flames were snuffed out, and the projectiles were scattered to the winds.

On the other side of the Great Hall, a white flame expanded across the room, engulfing the roots. Light magic. The flame enveloped the roots, purifying them. The roots broke apart, crumbling into ash, which blew away on the wind.

"Oh, dear." Lust placed a hand on her cheek. "You destroyed my darlings. Now what should I do? Oh! I know!"

Lust pointed a finger at Enyo and lightning burst from the tip, traveling at her faster than she could react. Jacob threw Durandal, infused with his energy, in front of Enyo. The lightning changed course, attracted by the new magnetic focus.

Bereft of his weapon, Jacob slammed his fist into the ground. A large pillar jutted up in front him. He kicked it, sending the object flying at Lust. It was destroyed, naturally, but Jacob had used it as cover to close the distance between them.

Giggling as she spotted him, Lust swung her blade, unleashing a torrential wave of dark magic. With his left hand, Jacob punched at the attack, releasing his own energy to cancel hers. Pain flared in his knuckles, but he ignored. Jacob closed the distance, and then struck Lust, impaling her with his hand.

Lust turned into mud.

"What?!"

Agony seared into his back. Blood dripped onto the floor. Gritting his teeth as he pushed past the pain, Jacob rolled across the floor, leapt back to his feet, and spun around.

Lust stood behind him, grinning as she licked his blood off her fingers. "Delicious."

Jacob grimaced. This woman was enjoying herself far too much. He was no longer even sure why she'd started this war. Nothing she did made sense. It was like she was doing all this purely for her own amusement.

A shout resounded behind Lust. "Don't. Touch. My. Man!"

Lust turned her head. She received a face full of white magic for her trouble. The orb, a type of condensed ball of light, smashed into her and sent the woman flying. She screamed in pain as she tumbled along the ground, rolling across the floor until her back smashed into the steps that lead up to the dais.

Enyo rushed up to Jacob. "Are you all right?"

"I'm fine," Jacob said. Indeed, his back wound was already healing thanks to his Linked Energy Manipulation.

"I'm glad. I thought… I was worried when I saw her attack hit you."

Jacob wasn't sure what kind of attack it was, though it must have possessed some impressive cutting power. He'd encased his body in a layer of energy. It was enough to stop most attacks, be they magical or otherwise.

"Don't worry," he said. "I won't leave you."

Enyo smiled.

"That was a good hit," Lust mumbled as she climbed to her feet. Her left cheek was swollen and bruised, and blood dripped down the corner of her lips. Despite this, she was smiling. "I wonder where this power was before? Does standing by the hero's side give you more strength? Perhaps I should seduce him to my side and see if it does the same for me."

"Sorry," Jacob said, setting himself into a narrow sword stance. "I'm not into old hags."

Far from being upset by the insult, Lust laughed. "We'll see how long that strong front lasts. I'll enjoy breaking you."

"Not if I have anything to say about it," Enyo said before she started chanting. "Fuvis. Nubilus. Displodo."

An explosion of dark energy erupted beneath Lust's feet like a gout of flames. There was no heat. Black magic wasn't actual fire. It just acted like fire.

Jacob rushed forward, grabbed Durandal where it was impaled into the ground, and pulled it out. By then, the flames had dispersed when Erica swung her hand out, but Enyo was already in the process of finishing her next chant.

"Nox. Umbra. Dissulto."

A small sphere appeared in front of Enyo, rapidly growing until it was nearly half the size of a human. Enyo pushed the sphere forward. Despite how large it was, it shot across the Great Hall like a cannonball, slamming into Lust, who created a silver barrier in front of her. The ball exploded. Dark particles burst everywhere like the dying embers of a fire.

Enyo had already finished her next chant.

"Nox. Umbra. Moltus. Imperium."

The particles of darkness floating around Lust suddenly shifted. Lust eyed the dozens of tiny marble-sized orbs with amused arrogance. She didn't get the chance to speak because the spheres shot forward seconds later. They came in at different angles, different times, and different trajectories. However, they all had one common goal: to riddle her full of holes.

Jacob stood on the sidelines, watching. It quickly became apparent that these marble-esque creations of dark matter weren't simply projectiles. When one of them missed, it would curve around and attack again. When Lust put up a barrier, it would move around the barrier and attack from a different angle. Enyo was controlling them.

He glanced at Enyo. Sweat poured from her forehead, and her breathing was ragged. She'd hunched her shoulders in concentration, left hand outstretched as if it was the control being used to move the spheres.

She won't be able to keep this up for long.

A technique like this required a lot of concentration, more than most people had. Enyo was strong-willed and had an incredible capacity for magic. Her innate talent and dedication allowed her to succeed where most failed, but even she had her limits.

"Get ready," he told his sword.

"I'm always ready," Durandal shot back.

The spheres eventually stopped. With a final gasp, Enyo was forced to release her technique. Lust wore a malicious grin. She raised her hand, tendrils of lightning arcing from her fingertips as she prepared an attack.

She'd never get the chance to release it.

Jacob stomped on the ground, creating a large quake that knocked the woman off balance, forcing her to cease her attack. He then rushed forward. The gap between them was closed in a second.

He attacked her with a quick thrust that was dodged. This didn't discourage him as he spun around and launched another attack to cleave her right shoulder to her left hip.

Lust leapt backwards. Jacob followed.

"Such forceful attacks," Lust moaned as if experiencing ecstasy. She moved left. His slash was dodged, but he changed the angle of his swing and sliced a long cut along her arm. "You don't go easy, do you?"

"It's not in my policy to go easy on women when they attack me and my friends," Jacob said. "An enemy is an enemy."

"So rough and straightforward. I like that in a man."

"Then you'll love this."

Jacob dug into the ground with Durandal and pulled it into an upwards slash. Rocks and dust flew into Lust's face. She shrieked as it got into her eyes, causing her to stumble backwards as and raise her hand. Not one to miss out on this opportunity, Jacob tried to cut her head off her shoulders.

Lust caught Durandal. It tried to shock her, but somehow, Jacob was the one who ended up being jolted when something like lightning traveled through his body.

"You're fighting dirty," Lust said, her voice still laced with sexual overtones. "Dirty fighting is bad. I think you need to be punished."

Jacob leapt backwards as Lust swept her hand at him. A gust of wind tried to push him into a wall, but he cut through it with Durandal. Out of the corner of his eye, he noticed Enyo finishing her chant and sent a return attack at Lust. She blocked the wave of energy and laughed.

"Is that all you've got, hero?"

Jacob said nothing. He didn't need to. Enyo was finished chanting.

Lust never saw Enyo's attack coming until it was too late.

Blood splashed against the ground. Lust looked down, blinking at the golden spear piercing her chest. She looked up at him, and then turned her head toward Enyo.

"You should remember that I've already figured out how your magic works," Jacob said. "Steal might be a powerful magic that allows you to take the powers of others, but there's a limit to how much power you can take, and the more you use other people's magic, the more stress you're placing on your mind. After all, that magic you're using wasn't originally yours."

"Ah ha. Ah-ah-ha-ha-ha!" Lust's laugh was lyrical despite the blood trailing down her mouth. "So during the time between our last battle and now, you've created a countermeasure. You force me to use as much magic as possible, making my mind lag, and while I'm distracted, the Dark Lady attacks from behind. Bravo. Very good. However, don't think this means you've won. The fun is just getting started."

Lust tapped on the ground, which started to rumble. Pieces of soil crawled along the ground, congealing together like droplets of water that increased in size. A flat piece of earth soon became a hill. The hill became a head, then shoulders, and then arms and hands. Like a skeleton climbing from the abyss of the underworld, a massive monstrosity of dirt and rocks seemingly climbed out of the ground. It loomed over them, a gargantuan figure casting the world in shadow.

It was a golem.

"I didn't know she had that kind of magic," Jacob muttered.

"Now then," Lust said, sitting on the golem's head. "Let's see how you handle this."

The golem raised its hand. Jacob jumped back. The golem slammed it into the ground where Jacob had been standing. Cracks appeared along the already fragmented earth. Jacob hopped backwards several more times, slicing apart those rock shards that the attack kicked up.

On the golem's other side, Enyo created a massive spear of dark matter, which she sent hurtling at the golem—only for the spear to be smashed apart by a giant fist. Enyo was then struck by that same fist. Her scream sent fear racing through Jacob's heart. He couldn't do anything for her, however, because the golem had turned back around and tried to make a pancake out of him.

Jump left. Leap right. Roll forward.

The golem's hands were like the hands of an angry god. It crushed the ground wherever it landed, creating a hand shaped imprint. Gnashing his teeth together, Jacob waited until the hand landed next to him again, and then he slashed at it with Durandal. He felt a moment of resistance. Sparks flew. Then, like a knife cutting through a slice of cheese, the hand was sheared off.

"Marvelous!" Lust crowed. "To think you can cut something that's been infused with nearly all my magic! Truly! You are the greatest hero I've seen!"

This woman...

She wasn't even taking this seriously. Just listening to her praises pissed him off. It was like she was mocking him.

"Obscurim. Opscurum. Obscuritas." A chant echoed around the room. "Exidio. Excisio. Exscidium."

A wave of dark matter rushed over the ground, enveloping the golem up to the waist. Jacob leapt into the air as the rock-like creation wobbled precariously, the flames eating at its legs. Descending upon Lust like an avenging angel, he thrust his blade out, creating a giant beam of condensed chi that was shaped like Durandal.

"Hmph!"

The beam splashed harmlessly against a barrier. At the same time, the golem stamped on the ground, creating a massive gust that somehow snuffed out the intense black fire.

Seeing the mocking smile on Lust's face as she stared at him from behind the shield, Jacob snarled and poured more energy into his attack. Cracks appeared. They spread across the barrier, increasing with every second. Jacob's attack petered out before it broke. However, he had landed on the golem by then, and a single slash of his blade shattered it.

Lust was still grinning as she created a dark blade of energy once more, though he noticed it was fizzling. She was running out of magic. As they clashed, their blades striking together, Enyo created a massive spear out of light. While Jacob kept Lust occupied, she launched the spear at the golem.

The spear pierced the golem through the chest. It stumbled forward, throwing Jacob off. He flipped around and landed on his feet. Looking up, he watched as the golem broke apart, crumbled like a house of cards, and created a huge cloud of dust that obscured his vision.

When the cloud dispersed, Lust was nowhere to be found. He looked left. Then he looked right. It was as if she'd disappeared. Frowning, he glanced at Enyo, who looked as confused as he felt.

A shadow appeared on the floor behind her. Fear raced through his veins when Lust emerged from within the shadow.

"Behind you!" Jacob shouted.

It was a testament to her trust that she didn't turn around to look. She leapt away instead, to avoid whatever potential attack was coming her way. This allowed her to avoid impalement. Sadly, it didn't stop her from getting hurt.

Blood gushed from a wound that opened on her left side, drenching her clothes and legs. A gasp emerged from her throat as she fell to her knees. Her hands came up, holding the wound, crimson pouring between her fingers like a river.

Lust grinned as she pointed a hand at Enyo. Lightning sparked along her fingertips as she chanted. Time slowed.

In desperation, Jacob threw Durandal with all his might. The sword arched through the air as it soared at Lust, who batted it away with contemptuous ease. As the sword spun through the air, Enyo, with one last surge of strength, leapt up, grabbed Durandal, and, ignoring the pain that came from touching it as sparks flew off the handle, plunged the sword into Lust's chest.

The lightning skittering across Lust's hand died. She lowered it to her side, slowly, almost calmly. Looking down, she eyed the blade sticking in her chest, at the blood running down her body, staining her black dress. She looked up at Enyo, who had taken several steps back, steam wafting from her now burnt hands.

"W-well played," she muttered before falling backwards.

Jacob ran up to Enyo as she fell to a knee and placed a hand on her shoulder. "Are you okay?"

"I-I'm fine," Enyo said through grit teeth. "Holding Durandal hurt more than I thought it would."

"I meant the wound on your torso."

"Oh. That's fine. I'm healing it. It just hurts."

"I imagine it would," Durandal quipped from where he was sticking out of Lust's chest.

"Not helping," Jacob and Enyo said at the same time.

"Heh… you two are such a unique pair," a pained, raspy voice said. They looked at the body lying before them. Lust's chest rose and fell. More blood spilled out from around Durandal. It bubbled like a fountain. Even though she must have been in excruciating pain, she was smiling. "A hero and the destroyer of a Dark Lord, and the one who is supposed to have given birth to the next Dark Lord. He-he-he, I've never heard of something so absurd, so amusing. Thank you."

Jacob frowned as he stood up and walked over to Lust. "Why are you thanking us? I don't understand you."

"Few people do." Blood-stained teeth revealed themselves when she peeled back her lips. "I am old, Hero. I've lived for nearly six centuries. When you get to be my age, you fear boredom more than you do death."

Lust coughed. More blood welled up in her mouth, forcing her to turn her head and spit it out.

"When I… when I heard that the Dark Lady had gone off with the hero, I was so happy. It was the first time this has ever happened.

I-it was different. Interesting. Exciting. For the first time in several centuries, my blood began boiling."

Enyo had healed herself by this point. Her footsteps came from behind him as she walked up to stand by his side. He reached out. She grabbed his hand and laced her fingers through his.

Lust grinned as if she could see what they were doing, even though her eyes were dimming. "I wanted to amuse myself. I wanted to see how far I could take this, how far you would go. I wanted... something different... and maybe... maybe I also wanted a fitting end." Lust closed her eyes and sighed. "I can't think of a more deserving end than being slain by the two of you."

He and Enyo remained silent as Lust's breathing stilled, as her body relaxed. Another moment passed. Jacob reached out, clasped his fingers around Durandal's hilt, and pulled the blade free. The sword, perhaps sensing his emotions, remained silent.

"I don't like that she's smiling in death," Enyo said.

"Neither do I," Jacob admitted.

"I hate even more that I understand how she feels."

"I can't say the same. We humans generally don't live more than seventy years."

"I guess that's true." Enyo paused to look at him. "Does this mean it's over?"

Jacob thought about that for a moment before slowly nodding.

"Yeah," he said. "It's over."

EPILOGUE - RETURN HOME

Two months after the battle and Alyssium was still in the process of recovering. There was a lot that went into repairing the damage that had been done to the city, but of course, not everything could be repaired. Many people had lost their lives. They were still counting the number of fatalities. It seemed as if more dead were being found every day.

The Alyssium knights were working hard toward finding the survivors and rendering aid. The magicians who'd survived had built a makeshift hospital, where they worked alongside doctors to help heal the physical damage that had been inflicted upon Alyssium's citizens.

Nothing could be done to heal the scars on the people's hearts. Only time could heal that.

During that time, Enyo and Jacob helped out where they could. A lot of people were wary of them. It was understandable. Until this moment, Jacob had been considered a traitor and Enyo was a member of the Dark Clan. However, as time passed, Enyo and Jacob continued to help, finding people who'd been buried under rubble, healing them on the spot, and the people eventually accepted them, however warily.

It wouldn't change the ultimate outcome or Jacob's feeling toward these people, but it was something.

Jacob had worked his hardest to help save the people of Alyssium, not because he believed it was his duty, but to make up for his sin. Lust had attacked Alyssium because of him and Enyo. This was their fault, even if no one but the two of them knew it.

He and Enyo had their own problems to deal with during that time. Enyo hadn't been able to deal with Fellis's death for the longest time. She'd worked herself to exhaustion every day by saving people, so at night she would pass out before she could consider doing otherwise. Yet even that didn't stop the nightmares. Every night, Enyo would wake up screaming. Every night, Jacob would hold her as she fell asleep crying out her sorrow.

It would be a long time before she recovered from Fellis's death, though she stopped crying a week after the battle.

That morning, he and Enyo woke up to the rising sun shining through their window. The soft bed underneath them was so comfortable. He wished he could've fallen back asleep, but they had things to do. Opening his eyes, he looked down at Enyo, who was snuggling against his chest. Her naked body rested against his.

Last night was the first time they'd had sex since the battle. He hadn't wanted to push Enyo, or take advantage of her emotional state. The previous night was the first time that she had initiated anything.

Stroking her hair, he watched Enyo until she slowly stirred awake. It was adorable how the first thing she did was look up, her hair in disarray and her eyes half-lidded. She blinked several times. Her eyes slowly gained alacrity as she stared at him, and then, like clouds breaking apart after a storm, her face lit up in a small but wonderful smile.

"Morning," she mumbled as she leaned in, giving him a soft kiss that he was more than happy to reciprocate.

Jacob placed his hand against her cheek. She closed her eyes and leaned into his touch.

"How did you sleep?"

"Better," she sighed.

Jacob rubbed his thumb against her soft skin as Enyo hummed. He slid his hand to the back of her head, fingers threading through her soft, pink hair. Enyo didn't wait for him to pull her to him. She leaned in to give him another kiss.

Had this been any other day, he would have allowed this moment to escalate, to give into his desire. Today, they couldn't afford to.

"Today's the day," he said.

"Yeah," Enyo said softly. "We're leaving today, huh?"

"That's right. We should probably get ready."

"Right…"

Since they didn't have time to spend in bed, he and Enyo climbed out and got dressed. Jacob pulled on his pants, stepped into his boots, and threw on his shirt. He looked over at Enyo. She'd already put on her shorts, sleeveless shirt, and heeled boots. Her appearance reminded him of a pirate almost, especially after she strapped the daggers around her hips.

Exiting the room, the first thing that greeted them was Durandal trying to tell Listy a dirty joke. "Jack and Jill went up the hill and did it in the water. Jack slipped. His condom ripped, and they ended up having a daughter. What do you think? Isn't it great?"

Listy said nothing, but her right eyebrow was twitching.

"Stop bothering Listy with your foul jokes, D."

"Hmph! I don't want to hear anything from you, Partner. You kicked me out last night!"

"Enyo and I had private matters to attend to last night," Jacob said emotionlessly. "There was no way I was going to let you see that, you dirty old sword."

"How could you not let me watch? We're partners! Partners are supposed to share everything!"

"We're not sharing our sex life with you," Enyo said in a voice so dry deserts would have been jealous. "This is one matter where being Jacob's partner gets you nothing."

"Whatever happened to bros before hoes?"

Listy coughed into her hand. "Are you two ready to leave? Alice and Kindness are already waiting for you."

Jacob strapped Durandal around his shoulder. "We're ready."

"Then follow me."

The otherworld gate was located in the basement below the castle. It had, fortunately, been left unscathed during the battle, perhaps because it was located in a secure chamber several dozen meters beneath Avant Heim.

They stood within a massive room. It was round, making Jacob feel like they were stuck in a giant cylinder. Dark gray walls covered in cracks were lit up with fairy lamps. In the center of the room was the otherworld gate, a giant circular device made of steel and glowing with strange lights. Jacob couldn't say for sure, but for whatever reason, he thought that the device looked far too advanced to be something from this world.

In front of the otherworld gate was a podium, and a slot was situated in the center of that podium. It was the lock that the otherworld gate key went into.

Alice and Kindness were standing by the otherworld gate. Kindness was smiling, though it was tinged with melancholy. Alice's lips trembled, but there was a determined glint in her eyes, as if she was prepared to see this through to the end.

"Are you sure I can't convince you to stay?" Alice asked.

Jacob shook his head. "Enyo and I have spoken about this at length. I don't belong here, I never did, and Enyo no longer wants anything to do with this world."

Squeezing Jacob's hand, Enyo added, "We'd like to start anew. Given our history with this world, it would be hard to begin a new life here."

Alice took a deep breath, and then she smiled. It was a fake smile—the fakest one he'd ever seen from her. This parting hurt her, but that wasn't going to change his mind. Once upon a time, it might have, but now there was nothing left for him to consider.

"I hope… I hope you two have a happy live together," Alice said.

"Thank you," Jacob and Enyo said at the same time. Alice sighed.

Kindness came up and grabbed both of their conjoined hands. Her smile was a lot more vibrant than Alice's.

"Thank you for all of your help. You never owed us anything, but you agreed to lend us your strength anyway. I'll never forget you two for as long as I live."

"We'll never forget you either," Enyo said in a heartfelt voice. "I hope you'll be able to live a life free of war from now on."

"So do I," Kindness admitted.

Jacob looked around, a frown growing on his face. "I noticed that Freya isn't here."

"You know how she is," Alice said with a sigh. "That woman can never stay in any one place for too long."

Jacob nodded. "True."

There was little left to be said. Kindness placed the otherworld gate key into the lock, twisting it. The podium lit up. Strange symbols appeared on a spot that had originally been blank. They reminded him of the computer graphics back in his old world, though he didn't recognize the symbols being shone. Soon enough, the otherworld gate lit up as well, glowing a light blue as a sphere of crackling energy appeared within the gate's center. It expanded, swelling until it fit in the circle like a ball inside of a ring. Then it flattened.

An image had appeared. It was blurry. Jacob could barely make it out, but what he saw was enough. The shapes of the buildings, even in their blurriness, were easily recognizable.

He looked at Enyo. "Are you sure about this? There's no telling if this will work, you know."

"I know." Her grip on his hand tightened. "And I'm sure. Just make sure you don't let go of me."

"Never," Jacob agreed.

Their goodbyes already said, Alice, Kindness, and Listy stepped away. He and Enyo took in a deep breath as they stared at the gateway that led to his world.

As one, they stepped into the portal.

Jacob wasn't sure if he could describe how it felt stepping through the otherworld gate. The hairs on his neck prickled, his skin broke out into goosebumps, and his eyesight became filled with white. There was a strange sense of weightlessness that made his stomach drop into his feet. For a moment, he was worried about falling into an abyss.

Then it was all over. The world returned to normal, but it was not the world that he'd spent the last several years in.

He was standing in an alley, large walls looming above him on either side. Sights, sounds, and scents that were nostalgic but no longer familiar filled his nose. Outside of the alley, people dressed in clothing far different from the one's living in Terrasole walked past the gap.

The hand that he held was shaking.

"J-Jacob?"

He turned his head. Enyo was still with him, still there. He breathed a sigh of relief, but then he saw the wide-eyed look on her face. She was in shock.

"I-is this…?"

"Yes," Jacob said. "I believe we've made it."

"Oh…"

Enyo looked around, blinking several times. Then she pinched herself.

"What are you doing?"

"Making sure I'm not dreaming."

"Uh-huh…" Since it looked like Enyo wasn't going to be moving anytime soon, Jacob tugged her along. "Come on."

Enyo walked slightly behind him, still dazed, as he led her out of the alley and into the sun. He was blinded for a moment. A feminine gasp told him that Enyo wasn't. He blinked the spots from his vision, and then looked around.

The road was paved black. People wearing familiar but strange clothes walked across the sidewalk—business suits, shorts, sneakers, baseball caps, and so on. Large contraptions on four wheels drove down the street, similar to chariots but so completely different. Signs written in a different language than Terrasole's sat against buildings that were too symmetrical to have been crafted by hand. Enyo looked at all of this with eyes that reminded him of a child's.

"Jacob… those chariots are moving without a horse."

"Those aren't chariots. Those are cars."

"Cars?"

"That's right."

"Those are the things you told me about before, aren't they?"

"They are."

"Oh..."

Jacob looked at all the people walking past them. In return, the people looked at him and Enyo oddly, probably because of their strange clothes and Enyo's unusual appearance. Pointed ears, pink hair, and pink eyes were not natural in this world.

He glanced back at Enyo. She was still clearly shocked, still letting her head twist around like she didn't have a spine.

"Jacob?"

"Yes?"

Enyo looked at him, vestiges of panic in her eyes. "I've been dreaming of this day for so long, of leaving my old world behind for a new one, of living a new life with you."

"I sense a 'but' coming."

"But now that it has actually happened, I don't know what to do," she confessed. Her eyes shook as she held his gaze, seeking reassurance in this strange world that she knew nothing about. "Jacob, what... what do we do now?"

He loved how she said "we."

Turning around so he was facing Enyo, he took her hands in his and held them to his chest. He gave her a reassuring smile before kissing her on the lips. When he pulled back, he looked into her eyes, which had calmed down and said...

"Now? Now all we have to do is live."

-Fin...

AFTERWORD

Hey everyone. If you are here, then it means you have finished my two volume light novel series, Journey of a Betrayed Hero. I want to thank everyone who read this story. I hope you all enjoyed it. However, I now have a confession to make.

It was brought to my attention that my previous volume had a lot of errors in it. Well, I looked at my book again, and I realized something really embarrassing.

I used the wrong manuscript.

I think I accidentally uploaded the rough draft instead of the final copy, so what everyone got was basically unedited and raw.

I am very sorry. I cannot even begin to apologize enough for this mistake.

I have since uploaded the correct manuscript for both kindle and paperback. If you bought the paperback on Amazon, you can download a FREE kindle copy using the kindle matchbook. If you bought the kindle version, you should be able to update your current version.

Saying that, it's not like the story itself is any different from the original. It just has better grammar and a few problem areas with story continuity were fixed.

There isn't much to say about this series. The story for Journey of a Betrayed Hero was very short and to the point. I didn't add any RPG, harem, or side story elements like most isekai because I felt like they would detract from my story and make it longer than it needed to be. I usually write long series, so this short and sweet story is very different from what I'm used to, but I think it was a good exercise to try something different.

Once again, I would like to thank my artist for helping me complete this. Aisoretto was literally the third artist I hired to help me out here. I really love his artwork. It has a very light novel aesthetic, which I believe works well for this particular series.

I also want to thank my editor and proofreaders. This version of the manuscript IS the actual edited version, so there is no need to say anything more. While I'm certain some errors will always slip through the cracks, I'm confident this one reads better than my last volume did when I first published it.

Finally, I would like to thank you readers for being so awesome and buying my books! If I wasn't an introverted nerd with a fear of people, I'd give all of you a big hug!

Before I go, I just wanted to ask if everyone who enjoyed reading this story could leave a review. You don't have to, but every review helps put this book in front of more readers.

Thank you all, and I hope you will be around to read whatever stories I publish next!

~Brandon Varnell

WIDEREBURT: LEGEND OF THE REINCARNATED WARRIOR

Chapter 1: The Final Battle

The air burst all around me. Flames seared the hair off my arms and caused my skin to crack and burn. Blood seeped from my skin, looking almost like lava leaking from cracks in the earth's crust.

Though I quickly circulated my Spiritual Power, channeling the water element through my body to heal my wounds, I did not allow myself to sigh in relief. More explosions were detonating all around me, forcing me to swerve in every direction. What's more, by channeling the water element and using it to heal myself, I had been forced to split my attention two ways.

The lightning covering my body had grown weaker as a result of my split attention. In that moment, seven figures appeared above me. I glared up at the winged beasts flying over my head. They were naughty but shadows. However, those shadows were currently surrounded by intense Spiritual Auras that crashed into me like tidal waves rolling over a small village.

One of those great beasts released an avian cry before it swooped down, and the moment it did, the blazing heat surrounding my body grew even more fierce. Sweat broke out on my skin. It quickly dried up under this unfathomable heat. I could feel my skin getting singed once more, and I knew that I could no longer afford to run.

Since this creature was using fire, I decided to use water.

Dissipating the lightning in my body, I took a deep breath, and then circulated my Spiritual Power again. Instead of the sensation of static crawling across my skin, something soft and almost gel like covered my body. One step further. Grimacing as the heat from the creature closing in caused steam to rise from my body, I channeled more Spiritual Power into myself and transformed my entire body into water.

The great beast was finally upon me. What had appeared was an avian of such immense size that even the dragons living in the Misty Mountain Range could not compare to it. Wings of orange and red fire flapped, causing heat waves to distort the air. Colorful designs ran along its body. It was a mixture of red, orange, yellow, and blue. Its plumage was a brilliant white that burned like an illuminating flame. Red and yellow tails trailed behind it as though simulating the ends of a shooting star. Intense crimson eyes glared at me with a hatred that I knew was mutual.

Gnashing my teeth together, I turned around, tucked my fist into my torso, and put all of my Spiritual Power into my next attack.

The beast drew near. I waited until the last second. Then I quickly spun around, dodging the beast by a hair's breadth. It was so close that my body, currently composed entirely of water, was beginning to boil. However, I did not let myself get distracted. Thrusting out my fist, I channeled my Spiritual Power through it and created a massive spike of water that extended from my arm.

Even though the intense heat from the flames surrounding this creature was immense, I was no weakling myself. Water evaporated and created waves of billowing steam. Even so, the spear held firm, refusing to dissipate, and it soon penetrated the beast's chest. Rather than spewing blood, what emerged from the creature was a bright white flame.

As the beast cried in pain, I immediately retracted myself and prepared to attack again.

That was when one of the other beasts swooped down. I saw the shadow and sensed the intent to kill me and quickly moved away. Once I had reached what I deemed a safe distance from the firebird, I released my control over water and transformed into lightning again. Everything around me immediately sped up, allowing me to safely jump several dozen meters in less time than it took to blink.

The bird that had swooped past me was just as massive as the firebird, but instead of being coated in flames, this one had green and white feathers. Its soft feathers gave it a very gentle appearance. However, I knew from the thousands of razor sharp cuts I'd received during my earlier engagement that I couldn't underestimate its deceptively soft appearance. A long tail moved behind it like a tassel. If I looked closely, I could see the atmosphere around it being cut by thousands of wind blades.

A loud crash caused me to cast my gaze toward the ground. Flames spewed from the ground down below as the fire bird crashed into the forest. I felt a sense of grim satisfaction as the creature shrieked in agony. Brilliant white flames, the lifeblood of that great beast, were spewing from its chest like a fountain.

I did not have much time to admire my handiwork, for the green bird released a sharp cry before charging at me. Knowing that my element was weak against this creature that could control the wind, I used Flash Step Version 3: Lightning Step to move away as quickly as I could, but the beast remained stuck on my tail, creating a vacuum that cut through the atmosphere to increase its speed.

Frowning, I once more split my attention. I didn't do much this time. Channeling the light element into my finger, I took careful aim and sent a condensed beam of light at the wind bird. What I got in return was a satisfied shriek as my attack sheared through one of its wings. Greenish white blood spewed from the area where the limb had been severed. Without both wings, it was unable to maintain flight and fell to the ground below.

However, just like before, I was given no time to celebrate my success. Five other birds had just descended. Each one was just as big as the previous two. Each one possessed the ability to control a different element.

A powerful beam of light slammed into me without mercy, burning my back as it sent me sailing toward the ground. My scream was lost to the wind. My body felt like it was being thrown into the Sun. Everything hurt. However, I did my best to shunt aside the pain, increased the flow of lightning through my body, and rolled out from underneath the powerful beam of light.

The beam continued on. It struck the side of a mountain several kilometers below. An explosion so massive that the wind buffeted me despite its distance went up, sending plumes of smoke and rubble into the sky. When the attack died down, the mountain was gone. In its place was a crater so large I was sure it would be visible even if I moved beyond this planet's atmosphere.

"Damn..."

I looked at the result of that attack, and then turned back to glare at the beast who'd caused it. The massive bird flapped its wings as it glared back. This creature looked like it was made of pure light, a combination of white and yellow feathers that appeared both soft and translucent. Yellow eyes glowed with a power that seemed almost divine.

While the bird and I entered a glaring contest, an intense killing intent slammed into me, forcing me to swerve from the spot where I'd been floating.

Six spheres made of water flew past the spot where I'd been. They slammed into the ground far below. Each sphere created a crater that easily spanned ten or fifteen meters across.

I could not admire this attack, for the moment I dodged it, I was forced to move again. This time, seven blades of darkness cut through the air. They were nothing more than black ripples. I swerved over one of them, and then flew down to avoid another. Twisting my body, I managed to avoid two more, but the last one had been aimed at where I would be rather than where I was.

"HA!"

Channeling light into my palm, I slammed it into the blade of darkness, causing the air around me to crackle as arcs of light and dark Spiritual Power raced across the sky. Gritting my teeth as the dark blade pushed me back, I released a furious cry and poured even more Spiritual Power into my palm. The dark blade exploded as I finally tore through it.

The creature that had released this was a bird made from darkness so pure it was like a black hole. Sharp wings covered its body. The only part of it that wasn't black was its eyes, which were pure white and contained no pupil. Alongside it was a bird with blue feathers, one with yellow feathers, another with brown feathers, and the light bird that had attacked me earlier.

I took a heavy breath as sweat poured from my brow. However, I knew I couldn't stop. Without even trying to recover, I released the restraints on my Spiritual Power. My body became energized as though the last several hours had never happened. I could feel the Spiritual Power coursing through me like a tempest. Light mixed with water and lightning inside of me, some of which leaked out because my body simply couldn't withstand the power output.

"Dammit... I had been hoping to save this for your boss," I muttered in a bitter voice.

Whether or not the five elemental birds heard me, they certainly knew that my threat level had suddenly increased. All five of them screeched as they gathered their own Spiritual Power. It congealed around their mouths, forming spheres of condensed energy. Barely a second had passed before they launched their attacks. Five beams of water, lightning, light, darkness, and earth flew toward me.

I did not meet their attacks head on. I wasn't stupid.

Using the power of light, I immediately vanished from the spot where I'd been standing. Their attack went through my after image. I didn't give them a chance to be surprised. Reappearing several meters above the most troublesome of the five, I turned myself into a streak of light and descended before it realized what I was doing. I barely felt any resistance as my body blew a whole clean through the black bird.

Landing on the ground at almost the exact same instant I had moved from point A, I looked up to see that my attack had done what I intended. The black bird with powers over darkness now had a large hole in its chest. What's more, the edges were frayed and refused to heal. While darkness was the antithesis of light, the same was equally true.

"Kari, I still have no real grasp over your affinity, but it is only thanks to you that this was possible," I said to myself as I watched the massive bird slowly break into particles of darkness.

My attack enraged the four remaining birds, who quickly descended toward me. I didn't even need to use Spiritual Perception to feel their intent to kill me. Almost before I could even move, they had each launched their own attack. The four elements of water, light, lightning, and earth swirled around each other to create mixed beam of power so large it could engulf a small city.

But I was no longer there.

As their attacks slammed into the forest floor and caused even more damage to the environment, I was already in front of the water bird. I reached out with my hand and touched its head. The bird's eyes were crossed as it stared at me, but I just smiled at it. I'm sure my smile was quite cold.

The water bird lit up as I shoved as much lightning into it as I could. With a shriek so loud it was nearly inaudible, the bird lit up like fireworks during the Summer Solstice. Smoke soon rose from its body. However, it was too slow. This attack would kill it, but the other birds would get to me first.

Clicking my tongue, I raised my hand, which had turned into a five meter blade of lightning, and then I brought it down. My attack created a seam of light within the bird, a small line that appeared from its beak to its tail feathers. The bird peeled apart at the seam, the two halves almost gently falling away from each other before the elemental beast turned into water that rained upon the ground.

Barely a second had past before something sharp pierced my back. I couldn't even cry out in pain as the air was stolen from my lungs. The ground beneath and the sky above blurred past me in dull streaks. Gritting my teeth, I turned my head and found the enraged eyes of the light bird glaring at me. It had pierced my back with its beak.

"Don't think…" I struggled to raise my hand. "Don't think…" Light, lightning, and water swirled around my arm as I channeled all three elements. "Don't think this will be enough to do me in!!!"

With a roar of defiance, I crashed my fist into the light bird's beak. A loud cracking sound echoed from the beak as an incision line appeared. One incision became two, then two became three, four, eight, sixteen. It quickly multiplied before cracking underneath the power of my fist.

The bird immediately stopped flying as it thrashed and screeched in pain. However, the forward momentum it had generated was enough that I was not able to stop from flying until I generated enough force with my own Spiritual Power to stop myself.

Reaching behind my back after I had stopped moving, I pulled out what remained of the beak from my back and tossed it away. Warm blood spilled down my back. I ignored it as I eyed the three remaining elemental birds. The lightning bird, the wind bird, and the now injured light bird.

"Ha… ha… ha…"

My shoulders heaved as I glared at the birds. However, I didn't think my glare was very effective just then. The Spiritual Power flowing through me was fluctuating. The aura covering my body flickered in and out. I didn't reveal my thoughts, but I was swearing up a storm internally as my Spiritual Power started running dry.

This technique I was using wasn't complete yet. If I'd had time to finish it, then maybe I could have already ended this battle, but luck had not been on my side.

It looked like the birds were just about to renew their attack, and I myself was prepared to re-initiate hostilities, but all of us suddenly froze in place as an intense Spiritual Pressure filled the air. My breathing quickly grew heavier as sweat formed on my brow. It was a cold sweat. I tried to take in a breath, but the pressure was causing my lungs to struggle with the simple act of taking in oxygen. It felt like something was crushing them.

A figure had suddenly appeared in front of me. He was a luminous being more beautiful than the Sun, a creature of such incomparable beauty that even in my hatred, I could not deny there was not a single flaw to be found. Pure white robes covered his body. Long and silver hair flowed freely like a waterfall down his head all the way to his bare feet. His long, pointed ears were the clearest signs that he wasn't human.

He did not have a very muscular body. Indeed, I would have said his body was quite feminine. He was slender and willowy. However, I didn't let that fool me, and even if he had been a woman, I wouldn't have underestimated him like some people would have done.

Despite his beauty, there was something odd about this man. Every part of him seemed bright and divine—every part except his blood red eyes. They were a dark crimson that seemed tainted somehow. Furthermore, that dark aura surrounding him seemed to present a direct contradiction to his vibrant, almost divine appearance.

The man took a deep breath as he looked at the three birds. He surveyed them with a slight frown, and then quickly glanced at where I had killed the others. I wanted to move, to attack this man with everything I had, but some invisible force kept me in place.

Finally, he looked at me.

"**To think a half-blood like you was able to defeat four of my seven slaves,**" he murmured. "**You know I had enslaved these monsters specifically to kill you? Your powers are indeed great. Given enough time, you might even pose a threat to me. It seems trying to send enslaved Demon Beasts after you was a mistake. I should have just come myself.**"

"Great Overlord of the Seventh Plain…" My fists shook with barely restrained hatred as I stared at the being before me. "You took everything from me. My wife. My child. Everything. I have waited for this day, waited for the day I would finally face you again, for the day I would finally kill you."

The being before me, the one I called the Great Overlord of the Seventh Plain, chuckled as though I had said something amusing. It was a grating laugh, not at all like something I'd expect from such a feminine figure. His laugh caused the hair on my neck to prickle.

"**Had your wife not shielded you from me, she would not have died. She only has herself to blame.**" He paused, his head tilting as he stared impassively into my rage filled eyes. "**As for your daughter… I could not allow a human who possesses such divine blood to live. Had I not killed her, she would have become a threat.**"

"A threat?" I whispered. "We were just living peacefully when you attacked us unprovoked and without warning. We were no threat to you. You laid waste to our home, destroyed our civilization, and killed my family without even a hint of mercy or provocation."

The Great Overlord of the Seventh Plain snorted. "**You may not understand it now, but you are indeed a grave threat to me— no, you are perhaps the greatest threat to ever exist. What I did was necessary.**"

I didn't think the blood flowing through my veins could have run any colder than it already was, but I was wrong. It was like my blood had frozen over. Only a chilling coldness that seeped through my entire being remained.

"Necessary, you say?"

"**Yes. Necessary.**"

"Necessary… for what?"

"**To keep you from being able to interfere with my plans.**" The Great Overlord of the Seventh Plain spread his arms wide and chuckled again. "**Just look at what you have done. A half-blood who hasn't even learned to control even a tenth of his abilities has defeated four of my seven slaves, Divine-rank Demon Beasts capable of annihilating entire cities with a single attack, and you would have defeated all of them had I not intervened. I'd say this level of destruction warrants intervention.**"

I had no idea what this monster was talking about, but I was done listening. He had attacked my family for a reason as dumb as protecting himself? From what? It was true that I had been the one who awakened him, but I had never harmed him nor had any intention to. Had he never appeared attacked my city, never attempted to kill me, never murdered my daughter, we would have left him alone.

My hatred surged, allowing me to overcome the intense pressure that had been pushing down on me. I compressed the last remaining Spiritual Power in my body. The aura that had been covering me vanished. To the average eye, it would have looked like my power had disappeared.

The Great Overlord of the Seventh Plain narrowed his eyes.

Then I vanished.

It happened in a flash. I appeared directly behind my foe, thrusting out my fist in a punch that caused the air to burst. However, without even looking behind him, the Great Overlord of the Seventh Plain placed his hand in the direction of my punch, catching it. A shockwave erupted from the contact.

I was already moving.

Appearing on his left in a manner that was almost like teleportation, I launched a powerful kick. This was also blocked. I was undeterred. I appeared again and again, moving all around him at speeds so fast I left multiple afterimages in my wake. One. Two. Four. Sixteen. Yet no matter how many punches and kicks I threw, no matter how fast I pushed myself, this monster blocked each and every one of them as though it was easier than breathing.

Meanwhile, I was running on empty.

With the last of my strength, I released a vicious scream and channeled all my energy into my fist. A bright glow erupted from it. The air around it distorted. Ripples spread through the sky as though the fabrics of reality itself were being torn apart.

The Great Overlord's eyes finally widened. With something resembling panic, he threw out his own punch, which glowed in the same manner as mine but with a dark energy that seemed vile. The air exploded between us as one fought to overpower the other. I gritted my teeth and pushed as hard as I could, wrecking my body. Blood exploded from my arms as my capillaries burst, my muscles tore apart like they were made of soggy parchment, and I could feel my very life being drained.

I didn't care. It didn't matter if I died so long as I killed this man.

Perhaps it was because I was so focused that I didn't see the attack coming at me until it was too late. However, when a fist appeared out of nowhere, all I could do was swear. The attack hit me.

Pain overrode my ability to see, causing a white film to cover my eyes.

I think I must have passed out. When I came to, I was lying on my back, in the middle of a massive crater so large I couldn't even judge its size. The Great Overlord of the Seventh Plain was above me, a sword made of pure darkness grasped firmly within his right hand. He raised the sword and brought it down.

In a last ditch effort, I unleashed all of the Spiritual Power I had left, channeled it into my right hand, and met the blade with a punch. Our attacks struck each other. Light bent. Air warped. Lightning crackled. The area around our mutual attacks became distorted as strange cracks appeared in the atmosphere like the gaping maw to a bottomless abyss.

An explosion suddenly rent the air as the world around me was torn apart. The last thing I saw before darkness engulfed me was the Great Overlord's surprised crimson eyes.

To read more of WIEDERGEBURT: Legend of the Reincarnated Warrior, go to my Patreon and sign up at https://www.patreon.com/ BrandonVarnell

Hey, did you know?
Brandon Varnell has started a Patreon
You can get all kinds of awesome exclusives Like:

1. The chance to read his stories before anyone else!
2. Free ebooks!
3. exclusive SFW and NSFW artwork!
4. Signed paperback copies!
5. His undying love!
Er... maybe we don't want that last one, but the rest is pretty cool, right?

To get this awesome exlusive conent go to:
https://www.patreon.com/BrandonVarnell
and sigh up today!

American Kitsune

volumes 1-10
are available now!

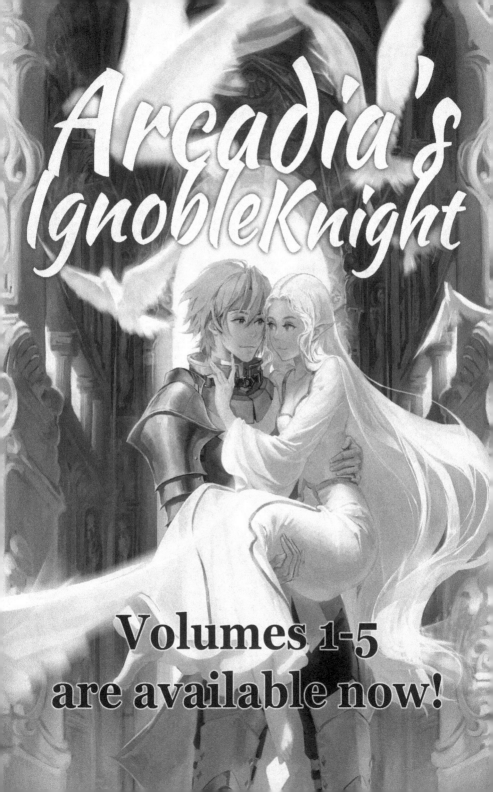

A
Most
Unlikely
Hero

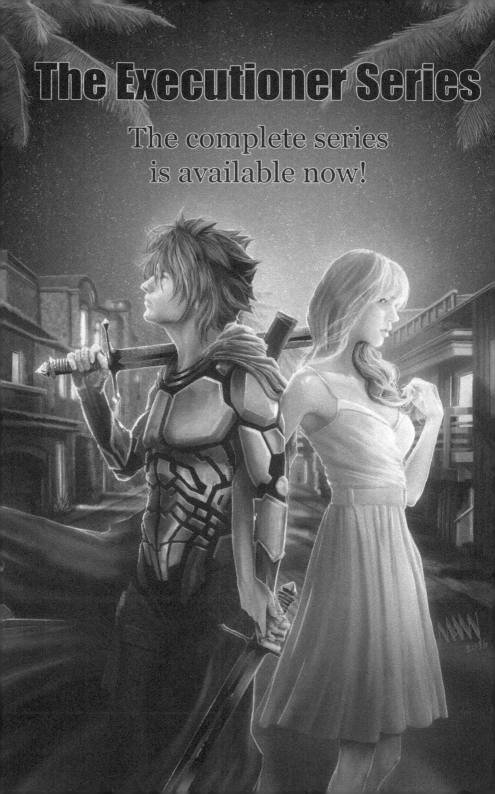

The Executioner Series

The complete series
is available now!

RIFT WARS: ORIGINS

Coming soon!

Swordsman Of the Rift

Author
Brandon Varnell

Artist
Lonwa A

Want to learn when a new book comes out?
Follow me on Social Media!

 @AmericanKitsune

 +BrandonVarnell

 @BrandonBVarnell

 http://bvarnell1101.tumblr.com/

 Brandon Varnell

 BrandonbVarnell

 https://www.patreon.com/
BrandonVarnell